THE MANUAL OF THE
CHRISTIAN KNIGHT

ERASMUS

AETERNA PRESS

PUBLISHED BY AETERNA PRESS.
COVER DESIGN BY AETERNA PRESS.

A BOOK CALLED IN LATIN ENCHIRIDION MILITIS CHRISTIANI AND IN ENGLISH THE MANUAL OF
THE CHRISTIAN KNIGHT REPLENISHED WITH MOST WHOLESOME PRECEPTS MADE BY THE
FAMOUS CLERK ERASMUS OF ROTTERDAM TO THE WHICH IS ADDED A NEW AND MARVELLOUS
PROFITABLE PREFACE

METHUEN & CO. 36 ESSEX STREET W.C. LONDON

THIS EDITION WAS FIRST PUBLISHED IN 1905

ISBN-13: 978-1-78516-151-3

AVAILABLE AS AN E-BOOK:
WWW.AETERNAPRESS.COM

CONTENTS

THE BOOK SPEAKETH

To please all sorts of men I do not pass,

To please the good and learned is a fair thing,

Yea, and these both were more than covenant was

And more than I look for. Whoso the learning

Of Christ doth favour, if he like well all thing

I seek no further, Christ is mine Apollo,

Only strengthening me to speak this that I do.

THE PRINTER TO THE FAITHFUL READER

THE mortal world a field is of battle

Which is the cause that strife doth never fail

Against man, by warring of the flesh

With the devil, that alway fighteth fresh

The spirit to oppress by false envy;

The which conflict is continually

During his life, and like to lose the field.

But he be armed with weapon and shield

Such as behoveth to a christian knight,

Where God each one, by his Christ chooseth right

Sole captain, and his standard to bear.

Who knoweth it not, then this will teach him here

In his brevyer, poynarde, or manual

The love shewing of high Emanuell.

In giving us such harness of war

Erasmus is the only furbisher

Scouring the harness, cankered and adust

Which negligence had so sore fret with rust

Then champion receive as thine by right

The manual of the true christian knight.

ENCHIRIDION

THE EPISTLE

ERASMUS OF ROTERDAME SENDETH GREETING TO THE
REVEREND FATHER IN CHRIST (AND LORD) THE LORD
PAUL WOLZIUS, THE MOST RELIGIOUS ABBOT OF THE
MONASTERY THE WHICH ISCOMMONLY
CALLED HUGHES COURT.

ALBEIT, most virtuous father, that the little book, to the which I have given
this name or title Enchiridion militis christiani, which many a day ago I made
for myself only, and for a certain friend of mine being utterly unlearned, hath
begun to mislike and displease me the less, forasmuch as I do see that it is
allowed of you and other virtuous and learned men such as you be, of whom
(as ye are indeed endued with godly learning, and also with learned godliness) I
know nothing to be approved, but that which is both holy and also clerkly: yet
it hath begun well nigh also to please and like me now, when I see it (after that
it hath been so oftentimes printed) yet still to be desired and greatly called for,
as if it were a new work made of late: if so be the printers do not lie to flatter
me withal. But again there is another thing which oftentimes grieveth me in
my mind, that a certain well learned friend of mine long ago said, very properly and sharply checking me, that there was more holiness seen in the little book
than in the whole author and maker thereof. Indeed he spake these words in
his jesting bourdyngly, but would to God he had not spoken so truly as he
bourded bitterly. And that grieveth me so much the more because the same
thing hath chanced to come likewise to pass in him, for the changing of whose
manners principally I took upon me this labour and travail, for he also not
only hath not withdrawn himself from the court, but is daily much deeper
drowned therein than he was aforetime, for what good purpose I cannot tell,
but as he confesseth himself with much great misery. yet for all that I do not
greatly pity my friend, because that peradventure adversity of fortune may
teach him once to repent himself, and to amend, seeing that he would not
follow and do after my counsel and admonitions. And verily though I, enforc-

ing me to the same thing and purpose, have been turned and tossed with so many chances and tempests, that Ulixes a man living ever in trouble (which Homer speaketh of) might be counted in comparison to me even Polycrates, ever lived in prosperity Without any manner trouble. I do not utterly repent me of my labour, seeing it hath moved and provoked so many unto the study of godly virtue: nor I myself am not utterly to be blamed and rebuked although my living be not in all points agreeing to mine own precepts and counsels. It is some part of godliness when one with all his heart desireth and is willing to be made good and virtuous: nor such a mind so well intending I suppose is not to be cast away, although his purpose be not ever luckily performed. To this we ought to endeavour ourselves all our life long, and no doubt but by the reason that we so oftentimes shall attempt it, once at the last we shall attain it. Also he hath dispatched a good piece of a doubtful journey which hath learned well of the journey the way. Therefore am I nothing moved with the mocks of certain persons which despise this little book, as nothing erudite and clerkly, saying that it might have been made of a child that learned his A, B, C, because it entreateth nothing of Duns's questions: as though nothing without those could be done with learning. I do not care if it be not so quick, so it be godly: let it not make them instruct and ready to disputations in schools, so that it make them apt to keep Christ's peace. Let it not be profitable or helping for the disputation in divinity, so it make for a divine life. For what good should it do to entreat of that thing that every man intermeddleth with? Who hath not in handling questions of divinity, or what else do all our swarms of schoolmen? There be almost as many commentaries upon the Master of the Sentence as be names of divines. There is neither measure nor number of summaries, which after the manner of apothecaries mingle oftentimes sundry things together, and make of old things new, of new things old, of one thing many, of many things one. How can it be that these great volumes instruct us to live well and after a christian manner, which a man in all his life cannot have leisure once to look over. In like manner as if a physician should prescribe unto him that lieth sick in peril of death to read Jacobus de partibus, or such other huge volumes, saying that there he should find remedy for his disease: but in the meantime the patient dieth, wanting present remedy wherewith he might be holpen. In such a fugitive life it is necessary to have a ready medicine at the hand. How many volumes have they made of restitution, of confession, of slander, and other things innumerable? And though they boult and search out by piece-meal everything by itself, and so define every thing as if they mistrusted all other men's wits, yea as though they mistrusted the goodness and mercy of God, whiles they do prescribe how he ought to punish and reward every fact either good or bad: yet they agree not amongst themselves, nor yet sometimes do open the thing plainly, if a man would look near upon it, so much diversity both of wits and circumstances is there. Moreover although it were so that they had determined all things well and truly, yet besides this that they handle and treat of these things after a barbarous and unpleasant fashion, there is not one amongst a thousand that can have any leisure to read over these volumes: or who is able to bear about with him Secundam secunde, the work of St Thomas? yet there is no man but he ought to use a good life, to the which Christ would that the way should be plain and open for every man, and that not by inexplicable crooks of disputations, not able to be resolved, but by a true and sincere faith and charity not feigned, whom hope doth follow which is never ashamed. finally let the great doctors, which must needs be but few in comparison to all other men, study and busy themselves in those great volumes. And yet nevertheless the unlearned and rude multitude which Christ died for ought to be provided for: and he hath taught a great portion of christian virtue which hath inflamed men unto the love thereof. The wise king, when he did teach his son true wisdom, took much more pain in exhorting him thereunto than in teaching him, who should say that to love wisdom were in a manner to have attained it. It is a great shame and rebuke both for lawyers and physicians that they have of a set purpose, and for the nonce, made their art and science full of difficulty, and hard to be attained or come by, to the intent that both their gains and advantage might be the more plentiful, and their glory and praise among the unlearned people the greater: but it is a much more shameful thing to do the same in the philosophy of Christ: but rather contrariwise we ought to endeavour ourselves with all our strengths to make it so easy as can be, and plain to every man. Nor let not this be our study to appear learned ourselves, but to allure very many to a christian man's life. on and ordinance is made now for war to be made against the Turks, which for whatsoever purpose it is begun, we ought to pray not that it may turn to the profit of a few certain persons, but that it may be to the common and general profit of all men. But what think you should come of it, if to such of them as shall be overcome (for I do not suppose that they shall all be killed with weapons) we shall lay the works of Occam, Durandus, Duns, Gabriell, Alvaros, or any such schoolmen, for the intent to bring them in mind to take Christ's profession upon them? What shall they imagine and think in their minds (for surely even they, though they be naught else, are men and have wit and reason) when they shall hear those thorny and cumbrous inextricable subtle imaginations of instances, of formalities, of quiddities, of relation: namely when they shall see these great doctors

and teachers of religion and holiness so far disagreeing, of so sundry opinions
among themselves that oftentimes they dispute and reason so long one with
another, until they change colour and be pale, and revile one another, spitting
each at other and finally dealing buffets and blows each to other. When they
shall see the black friars fight and scold for their Thomas, and then the grey
friars matched with them, defending one the other party their subtle and
fervent hot doctors, which they call Seraphicos, some speaking as Reals, some
as Nominals. When they shall also see the thing to be of so great difficulty that
they can never discuss sufficiently with what words they may speak of Christ:
as though one did deal or had to do with a wayward spirit which he had raised
up unto his own destruction, if he did fail never so little in the prescribed
words of conjuring, and not rather with our most merciful Saviour, which
desireth nothing else of us but a pure life and a simple. I beseech thee for the
love of God shew me what shall we bring about with all these reckonings,
specially if our manners and our life be like to the proud doctrine and learning? if they shall see and well perceive our ambition and desirousness of honour by our gorgeousness, more than ever any tyrant did use: our avarice and
covetousness by our bribing and pollyng, our lecherousness by the defiling of
maidens and wives, our cruelty by the oppressions done of us? With what face
or how for shame shall we offer to them the doctrine of Christ which is far
away contrary to all these things. best way and most effectual to overcome and
win the Turks, should be if they shall perceive that thing which Christ taught
and expressed in his living to shine in us. If they shall perceive that we do not
highly gape for their empires, do not desire their gold and good, do not covet
their possessions, but that we seek nothing else but only their souls' health and
the glory of God. This is that right true and effectuous divinity, the which in
time past subdued unto Christ arrogant and proud philosophers, and also the
mighty and invincible princes: and if we thus do, then shall Christ ever be
present and help us. truly it is not meet nor convenient to declare ourselves
christian men by this proof or token, if we kill very many, but rather if we save
very many: not if we send thousands of heathen people to hell, but if we make
many infidels faithful: not if we cruelly curse and excommunicate them, but if
we with devout prayers and with all our hearts desire their health and pray
unto God to send them better minds. If this be not our intent it shall sooner
come to pass that we shall degenerate and turn into Turks ourselves, than that
we shall cause them to become christian men. And although the chance of war,
which is ever doubtful and uncertain, should fall so luckily to us that we had
gotten the victory, so should it be brought to pass that the Pope's dominion
and his Cardinals' might be enlarged, but not the kingdom of Christ, finally

flourisheth and is in prosperity if faith, love, peace and chastity be quick and strong, which thing I trust shall be brought to pass by the good governance and provision of the Pope Leo the Tenth, unless the great trouble and rage of worldly business pluck him from his very good purpose another way. Christ doth profess to be primate and head himself in the heavenly kingdom, which never doth flourish but when celestial things be advanced. Nor Christ did not die for this purpose that goods of the world, that riches, that armour, and the rest of ruffling fashion of the world, be now in the hands and rule of certain priests, which things were wont to be in the hands of the gentiles, or at least amongst lay princes, not much differing from gentiles. But in my mind it were the best, before we should try with them in battle to attempt them with epistles and some little books: but with what manner of epistles? Not with threatening epistles, or with books full of tyranny, but with those which might shew fatherly charity, and resemble the very heart and mind of Peter and of Paul, and which should not only pretend and shew outwardly the title of the apostles, but which also should savour and taste of the efficacy and strength of the apostles. because I do not know that all the true fountain and vein of Christ's philosophy is hid in the gospel and the epistles of the apostles: but the strange manner of phrase, and oftentimes the troublous speaking of divers crooked figures and tropes be of so great difficulty, that oftentimes we ourselves also must labour right sore before we can perceive them. Therefore in mine opinion the best were that some both well learned men and good of living should have this office assigned and put unto them, to make a collection and to gather the sum of Christ's philosophy out of the pure fountain of the gospel and the epistles and most approved interpreters, and so plainly that yet it might be clerkly and erudite, so briefly that it might also be plain. Those things which concern faith or belief, let them be contained in a few articles. Those also that appertain to the manner of living let them be shewed and taught in few words, and that after such fashion that they may perceive the yoke of Christ to be pleasant and easy, and not grievous and painful: so that they may perceive that they have gotten fathers and not tyrants, feeders and not robbers, pyllers nor pollers, and that they be called to their soul health and not compelled to servitude. they also be men, neither their hearts be of so hard iron or adamant but that they may be mollified and won with benefits and kindness, wherewith even very wild beasts be waxen gentle and tame. And the most effectuous thing is the true verity of Christ. But let the Pope also command them whom he appointeth to this business, that they never swerve nor go from the true pattern and example of Christ, nor in any place have any respect to the carnal affections and desires of men. And such a thing my mind was about to bring to pass as well as I could, when I made this book of Enchiridion. did see the common people of Christendom, not only in effect, but also in opinions to be corrupted. I considered the most part of those which profess themselves to be pastors and doctors to abuse the titles of Christ to their proper advantage. And yet will I make no mention of those men after whose will and pleasure the world is ruled and turned up and down, whose vices though they be never so manifest, a man may scarcely once wince. And in such great darkness, in such great troublous ruffling of the world, in so great diversity of men's opinions, whither should we rather fly for succour than to the very great and sure anchor of Christ's doctrine, which is the gospel. being a good man in deed, doth not see and lament this marvellous corrupt world? When was there ever more tyranny? When did avarice reign more largely and less punished? When were ceremonies at any time more in estimation? When did our iniquity so largely flow with more liberty? When was ever charity so cold? What is brought, what is read, what is decreed or determined but it tasteth and savoureth of ambition and lucre? Oh how unfortunate were we if Christ had not left some sparks of his doctrine unto us, and as it were lively and everlasting veins of his godly mind. therefore we must enforce ourselves to know these sparks, leaving the coals of men's phantasies: let us seek these veins until we find fresh water which springeth into everlasting life. We delve and dig the ground marvellously deep for to pluck out riches, which nourisheth vice: and shall we not labour then the rich earth of Christ to get out that thing which is our souls' health? There was never no storm of vices that did so overcome and quench the heat of charity, but it might be restored again at this flint stone. is a stone, but this stone hath sparks of celestial fire, and veins of lively water. time past Abraham in every land did dig pits and holes, fetching in every place the veins of lively water: but those same being stopped up again by the Phylistyens with earth, and his servants did delve again, and not being only content to restore the old, did also make new. But then the Philistyans did scold and chide, yet he did not cease from digging. in this our time we have Phylistyans which do prefer the naughty earth to the lively fountains, even those which be worldly-wise, and have their respect to earthly things, and wring and wrest God's doctrine and his gospel to their carnal affections, making it serve to their ambition, bolstering up therewith their filthy lucre and tyranny. And if now any Isaac or any of his family should dig and find some true and pure vein, by and by they brable and cry against him, perceiving right well that that vein should hurt their advantage, should hurt their ambition, although it make never so much for the glory of Christ: straightway they cast in naughty earth, and with a corrupt interpretation they stop up the vein, and drive away the digger: or at the least they make it so muddy with clay and filthiness, that whosoever drinketh thereof shall draw unto him more slime and naughtiness than he shall good liquor. will not that those that thirst and desire righteousness do drink of the pure liquor, but they bring them unto their old worn and all too trodden cisterns, which have broken stones and mortar, but water they have none. But yet for all this the very true children of Isaac that be the true worshippers of Christ, must not be wearied and driven away from this labour: for verily even they which thrust naughty earth into the fountain of the gospel, would be counted the very worshippers of Christ. So that indeed nothing nowadays is more perilous than to teach truly Christ's learning, so greatly have the Philistyens prevailed fighting for their earth, preaching earthly things for celestial, and men's inventions for God's commandments: that is to say, not teaching those things which make for the glory of Christ, but those things which be for their own advantage, which be pardons, ons, and suchlike pilferings. And these they do so much more perilously because they cloke their covetousness with the titles and names of great princes, of the Pope of Rome, yea of Christ also Himself. But there is no man that doth more for the Pope's profit or business, than he that teacheth Christ's learning purely and truly, whereof he is the chief teacher. There is no man that doth more good to princes or deserveth more of them, than he which endeavoureth himself that the people may be wealthy and in prosperity. But some of the flock of schoolmen will here speak against me, saying it is easy to any man to give general precepts what is to be desired and what is to be eschewed: but what shall be answered then to those that ask counsel for so many fortunes and chances? First I answer that there be more divers kinds of such worldly business than that any living person can give direct and sure answer to each one of them. ly there is such diversity of circumstances, which if a man do not know, it is not well possible to make an answer. In conclusion, I doubt greatly whether they themselves have any sure answer that they may make, seeing they differ in so many things amongst themselves. And those also which amongst them be more wise than other do not thus answer: This ye shall do, this ye shall not do; but of this manner: This in mine opinion were the better, this I suppose to be tolerable. if we have that simple and bright eye which the gospel speaketh of, if the house of our mind have in it the candle of pure faith set upon a candlestick, all these trifles shall easily be put away and avoided as it were clouds or mists. If we have the rule and pattern of Christ's charity, to it we may apply and make meet all other things right easily. But what will ye do when this rule doth not agree with those things which hath been commonly used so many hundred years, and which be ordained and stablished by the laws of princes, for this thing chanceth very oft? Ye must not condemn that thing which princes do in executing their office, but again do not corrupt and defile the heavenly philosophy with men's deeds. Christ continue and abide, as he is indeed, a very centre or middle point unmoved, having certain circles going round about him: move not the mark out of his own place. which be in the first circle next to the centre (that is to say next to Christ) as priests, cardinals, popes, and such to whom it belongeth to follow the Lamb whithersoever he shall go, let them embrace and hold fast that most pure part, and so far forth as they may let them communicate and plenteously give the same unto their next neighbours. the second circle all temporal and lay princes be, which in keeping war and making laws, after a certain manner do service to Christ, either when with rightful battle they drive away their enemies and defend and maintain the public peace and tranquillity of the commonwealth: or else when with punishment according to the laws, they punish malefactors and evil-doers. And yet because they cannot choose but of necessity be occupied and busied in such things as be joined with the most vile dregs and filth of the earth, and with the business of the world, it is jeopardous lest they do fall further from the centre and mark, as lest they should make sometimes war for their own pleasure, and not for the commonwealth: lest under the pretext of justice they should use cruelty upon those whom they might reform with mercy: lest under the title of lordship they should pyll and polle those people whose goods they ought to defend. moreover as Christ like the fountain of everlasting fire, doth draw next unto him the order of priests, and maketh them of like nature, that is to say pure and clean from all corruption of worldly dregs and filthiness: so in like case it is the office of priests, and specially of the highest, so much as they can to call and draw unto them those that be princes and have power and authority. And if it fortune at any time that war do rise suddenly in any place, let the bishops endeavour themselves so much as in them is, either to end the strifes and variances without shedding of blood: or if that cannot be brought to pass, by reason of the great storms of worldly business, yet let them so do that as little blood as may be be shed, and that the war may shortly be brought to an end. In times past the bishops' authority had place even in just punishments, hath gotten divers times (as Saint Augustyne plainly in his epistle doth testify) the malefactor from the hands of temporal judges. For some things there be so necessary unto the order of the commonwealth, that partly yet Christ did dissemble at them, and partly he put them from him, and partly neither approving nor disallowing them did in a manner wink and look beside them. He would not know the money of Cesar, nor the scripture upon it. tribute he commanded to be paid if it were due and debt, as though it little pertained to him, so that God had his duty. The woman taken and found in adultery he neither condemned neither openly absolved, but only did bid her that she should no more do so. Of those which were condemned of Pylate, whose blood he intermingled amongst their sacrifices, he neither said it was well done nor evil, but only threatened every man that they should be punished with a like destruction if they did not amend. Moreover, when he was desired to divide the inheritance between the two brethren, he plainly refused it as an unworthy thing for him to give judgment of such gross matters, which did teach things heavenly. And also of the other part there be certain things which he openly abhorred, as the covetous Phariseys, hypocrites, the proud rich folks, saying unto them Woe be unto you. He never rebuked the apostles more sharply than when they would have been avenged, or when they were ambitious. When they asked him whether they should command fire to be sent down from heaven to have burned up the city from whence they were shut forth, he answered and said to them, Ye know not of what spirit ye are. When Peter was about to have called him unto the world from his passion suffering, he called him an adversary. When they contended about pre-eminence which of them should be the best, how often and how many ways doth he call them back to a contrary mind? other things there be which he teacheth and commandeth openly to be observed, as not to resist evil, to do good to thine enemies, to use meekness of mind, and other like. These must be departed in sunder, and every of them set in order in his own place. us not therefore straightway make Christ an author of all things which be done by princes and temporal officers, nor defend it (as we call it) to be done by God's law. They deal and meddle with many things which be low and gross, not altogether of the very pureness of a christian man: yet they be not to be rebuked inasmuch as they be necessary to the maintenance of order to be observed. Nor we be not by the ministering of their office made good, albeit that by them it is caused that we be less evil, and that they which be evil do less hurt and annoyance to the commonwealth. And therefore they also ought to have their honour because they do somewhat serve the justice of God and the public and common tranquillity, without the which sometime those things be troubled and vexed which belong to godly holiness. They must be honoured when they do their office: and if sometimes they use their power for their own pleasure or profit, yet peradventure it were the best to suffer them, more hurt should spring thereof: for there appeareth an image or rather a shadow of the divine justice in them, which justice yet ought to shine more evidently and more purely in the living and laws of priests. An image doth of another manner shew in a mirror of glass, than it doth in iron. in the third circle must all the common people be, as the most gross part of all this world, but not yet so gross but that they pertain unto the mystical body of Christ: for the eyes be not only members of the body, but also the legs, the feet, and the privy parts. And those which be in the third circle we ought so to suffer in their infirmity, that as much as is possible we do call them unto those things which be more approved of Christ. For in the mystical body he that but late was the foot may be the eye. And like as the princes if they be not all the best, must not with chiding be exasperate, lest (as Saint Augustyne saith) when they be moved they stir up more perilous tragedies, the weak people like as Christ suffered his apostles and nourished them, must be suffered, and after a fatherly manner cherished until they wax more aged and strong in Christ. For godliness also hath his infancy, it hath mean age, it hath full strength and perfect age. Yet all men after their degree must endeavour themselves to attain and come unto Christ. The elements have every one his proper place, but the fire which hath the highest place by little and little draweth all the other unto him, and so much as he can turneth them into his nature. clear water he turneth into the air, and the air clarified he transformeth into his own nature. Saint Paul doth in many things suffer and pardon the Corynthyans, but in the mean season putting difference between those things which he did proffer in the name of his Lord unto them that were perfect, and those things which he did pardon that were written in his own name to them that were yet weak and young in Christ: but ever on this trust that they should profit and go forward to more strength and perfection. And also he travaileth again to bring forth the Galathyans, until Christ be fashioned in them. Now if any man will think this circle to be more convenient for princes, I will not strive greatly with him. But whatsoever is without the third circle is at all times and in all points to be hated and refused, as ambition and desire of money, lechery, ire, vengeance, envy, backbiting, and such other pestilences, which then only be made incurable, when they disguised with the visor and cloak of holiness and virtue do creep into the circle afore spoken: that is when under the pretext of executing the law and justice we use our tyranny. When by the occasion of religion we provide for great lucre. When under the title of defending the church we hunt for worldly power and authority: and whensoever those things be commanded as things pertaining unto Christ which be disagreeing much from his learning. the mark must be set before every man which they ought to shoot at: and there is but one mark, which is Christ and his most pure learning. If thou set forth a worldly mark in the stead of a celestial mark, then shall there be nothing whereunto a man ought justly enforce himself, which laboureth to profit and go forward. man ought to enforce himself to that which is best and most perfect, that at the least we may attain and come to the mean things. And there is no cause why we should put away any kind or manner of living from this mark. The perfection of Christ consisteth only in the affections, and not in the manner or kind of living: it consisteth in the minds and not in the garments or in meats and drinks. There be among the monks which be scarce able to be put in the third circle, and yet I speak of those which be good, but yet weak and not perfect. There be amongst these that have had two wives which Christ thinketh worthy for the first circle. Nor yet in the mean time I do no wrong to any manner of living or profession, though I propound and set forth afore every man that thing which is best and most perfect: unless ye would think Plato to have done injury against all cities because in his book of the governing of a city or a common-wealth, he feigned such example of a commonwealth as yet never any man could see. Or except ye do think that Quintilian hath hurt the whole order of orators, because he feigned such an example of an orator as yet never was. And though thou be far from the principal and and chief patron Christ, thou art not yet therefore cast away, but stimulated and moved to go forward and profit. Art thou near the mark? Then art thou monished and counselled to approach more near: for there was never yet any man that went so far forward, but that he might have gone much more near the mark. There is no kind of living but it hath some perilous points annexed unto it, to cause men to degen-erate from the truth: and whosoever sheweth those jeopardous and dangerous points, doth not derogate or minish the honour of the order, nor speak against it, but rather is for the profit thereof. the felicity of princes is in danger to fall into tyranny, is in danger and jeopardy of foolishness and flattering, now whosoever sheweth those dangers to be eschewed, doth deserve thanks of the order of princes. Nor he doth not speak against their majesty, wherein they glory, which doth shew in what things their very majesty doth consist, which also doth put them in remembrance whereto they were sworn when they took their authority, what is their duty unto their people, and what they ought to do unto their officers. heads and rulers of the church have in a manner affinity with pestilent vices, avarice and ambition, which well perceiving St Peter the chief pastor next unto Christ, monish the bishops to feed their flock, and not to pyll, poll, and flay them: nor that they should not feed them because of any filthy advantage, but of their free and ready will: nor that they should use themselves as lords upon them, but that by the example of life, they should provoke them to godliness rather than by threatening and power. Doth he then speak against the order of priests which doth shew by what means, and how the bishops may truly be great, mighty, and rich? the kind of religious men is accompanied most commonly (besides other enormities) with superstition, pride, hypocrisy, and backbiting. doth not straight condemn their manner of living which doth shew and admonish them, in what things most true religion doth stand or rest, and how much the true godliness of a christian man is away from pride, and how far true charity is from all feigning and deceit: how much backbiting and slandering and venemousness of tongue is contrary to pure and true holiness. And specially if he shew what is to be eschewed after such sober and discreet manner, that he do neither name any man nor touch any order. thing is that in this mortal life so fortunate and prosperous, but hath some pestilent things annexed unto it? Therefore like as he doth not noye the health of the body but helpeth it, whosoever sheweth what things corrupteth health and what things preserveth it: so he doth not dissuade men from religion, but exhorteth them rather unto it, which sheweth the corrupt infections thereof and also the remedies. I am informed that there be divers which so judgeth of this book, as though the precepts thereof did withdraw and turn away men's minds from the life of religious men, because they do not so much praise and allow ceremonies, neither yet man's constitutions as some would, which indeed overmuch regard them. And there can be nothing so circumspectly spoken, but that thereof lewd and evil persons do take occasion either of quarrelling or else of sinning: that it is dangerous nowadays to any man to teach anything well. If a man should dissuade some such war and battle which now of long time hath been used, worse than was ever any amongst the gentiles, for things of no value, he should be noted by and by of the pick-quarrels to be one of those which thinketh that no war is lawful for a christian man. For these which were the bringers up and authors of this sentence we have made heretics, because a pope, I wot not who, doth seem to approve and allow war. yet he is not suspected nor noted of heresy, which doth provoke and stir up men to battle, and bloweth the trumpet thereunto for every trifling matter, against the doctrine both of Christ and of his apostles. If a man admonish that this is a deed truly belonging to the successor of an apostle to bring the Turks unto religion with Christ's help, rather than with war: anon he is suspected as though he affirmed not to be lawful for christian men to withstand the Turks, when they invade us. a man shew and praise the temperance that was in the apostles, and speak anything against the great superfluity that is used nowadays, he should be noted as a favourer of the Ebyonytes. And if a man did exhort diligently that these which be married should rather be joined together by the consents and agreeing of their minds, than by the embracings of their bodies, and so purely to use matrimony that as much as might be it were made like to virginity: he should be anon suspected to think that every act of matrimony were sin and un-lawful, as the Marcionytes did. If a man do admonish that in exercise and disputations, specially of divinity, there should be no ambitious pertinacity to overcome his fellow in defending his own opinions, nor no ambition to shew what they can do in commonplaces: he is wrongfully accused as though he did condemn utterly all school learning. Nor Saint Augustyne when he giveth warning to the logicians that they should beware of lust to brawl and chide, doth not condemn logic, but sheweth the pestilence thereof that it might be eschewed. he doth not dispraise virtue nor praise vice, which sheweth the preposterous and wrong judgment of the common people, which among virtues esteem those to be of most great value and chiefest which be of the lowest sort: and among vices most sore hateth and abhorreth those most small faults and trifles, and so contrariwise. Anon he is accused as though he should favour those vices which he sheweth to be more grievous than other, and as though he should condemn those good deeds and benefits to whom he preferreth other more holy and better. As if a man did admonish and give us warning, that it is more sure to trust unto good deeds than to trust to the pope's pardon, he doth not forsooth condemn the pope's pardons, but preferreth that which by Christ's learning and doctrine is of more certainty. if a man do teach those for to do better which tarry at home and provide for their wife and children, than those which go to see Rome, Hierusalem or Saint James, and that money which they should spend in that long and perilous journey to be better and more devoutly spent upon poor folks, yet condemneth not he their good intent, but preferreth that which is more near to very godliness. And this is a thing not only used now in our time but also in times heretofore past, to abhor some vices as though there were none other, fawning upon the rest as they were no vices at all, when in very deed they be more detestable than those which we so hate and abhor. Augustyne doth complain in his epistles that lasciviousness of the flesh is only imputed unto the priests of Affryke as a vice, and that the vice of covetousness and drunkenness be taken well nigh for a praise. This specially we speak most against, and cry out upon and exaggerate for an exceeding abominable fact, if one touch the body of Christ with the same hands wherewith he hath touched the body of a harlot. And there be some over-raging bold that be not afraid openly to affirm that it is less sin for a woman to commit carnal act with a brute beast than to lie with a priest. Now he that something rebuketh their shamelessness, doth not therefore favour the naughtiness of priests, but sheweth that they regard not those offences which be a great deal more to be cried out upon. if a priest be a dicer, a fighter, a brawler, all unlearned, drowned and wrapped in temporal business, all given to the evil service of evil princes, yet against him they cry nothing at all which altogether worldly and polluted doth handle and intermeddle with holy mysteries. a priest is a flatterer or a pick-quarrel, which with his bitter tongue and false lies doth hurt the names of those which never offended him, but rather hath done him pleasures, why do we not now cry out? Oh what an horrible sin is this to receive the Lord God, which suffered his passion for sinners, with that tongue which is full of poison of hell, and with that mouth wherewith thou killest and flayest an innocent. But this evil and ungraciousness we set so little by that in a manner those men are even praised for it, which profess themselves to be the most religious amongst religious men. There is no man that denieth but they be to be reprehended and sore rebuked which nourish and keep at home concubines, to the evil example of all the common people; but yet these other evil vices be more hateful to God. Nor he doth therefore say that butter is naught which sayeth that honey is better and more to be preferred: nor yet doth not approve the fever that counselleth the frenzy more to be avoided. And it is hard to tell and express how great infection of manners and disposition doth spring of these perverse and wrong judgments. be divers things nowadays received into the order of virtues, which rather have the visor and appearance of godliness than the nature and strength of it, insomuch that unless we look well into them and take good heed of them, they do quench and utterly destroy virtue. If it had been but a little pestilence of religion which in ceremonies do lie covert, Paul would never so sharply have spoken against them in all his epistles. yet do not we condemn in any place ceremonies that be moderately observed, but that all holiness be ascribed unto them we cannot suffer. Augustyne did prohibit those of the clergy which were in house with him to use any notable vesture, but if they would be commended of the people, that they should rather bring that to pass by their manners and virtuous living than by any sundry fashion of raiment. But nowadays it is a world for to see what new and wonderful fashions of apparel and vesture there be. yet I speak not against that, but this I marvel of, that those things are so overmuch regarded and set by, which peradventure might by right be reprehended. And again that those things be so little regarded which we should only behold and regard. I do not rail against the grey friars and black monks that they make much of their own rule, but because certain of them regard more their own rules than they do the Gospel: which thing would to God were not found in the most part of them. I do not speak against that, that some eat fish, some live with herbs, other with eggs: but I admonish those to err and to be far out of the way which will of those things justify themselves after the manner of the Jews, thinking themselves better, and preferring themselves to other for such trifles of men's invention, and take it for no default at all to hurt another man's good name with false lies. the diversity of meat and drink Christ never commanded anything, nor the apostles: but Paul oftentimes did dissuade us from it. Christ curseth bitter slandering, which also all the apostles doth detest and abhor: and yet that notwithstanding we will appear religious in such using of meats, and in hurting men's fame we be bold and hardy. I pray you think you that he which doth admonish these both in general not touching any man, and also lovingly, doth hurt religion? Who is so mad that he would be accounted eloquent for shewing and bringing to light the vices that belong to monks? But these peradventure fear lest their convents and brethren would be less obedient, and lest also there do not so many desire to be shaven into their order: yet verily, no man is more obedient to his head than he which inspired with the Holy Ghost is free and at liberty. True and very charity taketh all things well in worth, and suffereth all things, refuseth nothing, is obedient unto rulers, not only to those that be sober and gentle, but also to those that be sharp and rough. yet rulers must be wise of this that they do not turn the obedience of other men into their own tyranny, and that they had liefer therefore to have them superstitious than holy and virtuous, whereby they might be more obedient at every beck. They have pleasure to be called fathers: but what carnal father is there that would have his children ever infants and young because he might use his power upon them at his own pleasure? And of the other part all those that purpose to profit in the liberty of Christ, this they must be ware of, lest as Saint Paul doth admonish they make their liberty a cloke or covert to their carnal living: or as Saint Peter teacheth, with their liberty they make a cover and a cloke to their maliciousness. And if that one or two do abuse this liberty, yet it is not right forthwith that all other therefore be ever kept in superstitiousness and bondage of ceremonies like unto the Jews. And whosoever will mark it shall perceive that amongst these religious men, no man causeth the ceremonies to be more straitly observed than they which under the precepts thereof doth bear rule and serve their bellies rather than Christ. they need not be afraid lest such kind of Essenes be not enough spread abroad in so great diversity of men's natures, whereby it is caused that nothing is so unreasonable but divers and many will love and desire it, although theirselves ought more to desire that they had true professors of religion rather than many. But would to God that it were provided and ordained by a law that no man should be taken in such snares afore he were thirty years of age, before he something knew himself, or knew what the nature and virtue of true religion is. these which like unto the Phariseys, doing their own business and providing for their own profit, wander about to make novices both by sea and land, shall never fail of young men lacking experience whom they may allure into their veils and nets, and also deceive. There be a

great number of fools and simple souls in every place. But I desire even with all
my heart, and I doubt not but so do all that be very good men, that the religion of the Gospel should be so pleasant to every man that they being contented therewith, should not desire the religion of black monks or grey friars. And
I doubt not but so would Saint Benedicte and Fraunces themselves. did rejoice
that his own honour was defaced and dimmed with the glory of Christ: and so
should those other be glad if for the love of Christ's law we set nothing by
man's constitutions. I would that all christian men should so live that these
which now be called only religious, should appear little religious, which thing
even at this day is of truth and that in many: for why should I dissemble that
thing that is so manifest? yet in the old time the beginning of the monastical
life was nothing else but a going aside into a secret place from the cruelness of
idolaters. And anon after the manner of living of religious men which followed
them was nothing else but a reformation and calling again to Christ: for the
courts of princes in the old time shewed them christened in their titles rather
than in their living. The bishops anon after were corrupt with ambition and
covetousness, and the common people also fainted and waxed cold from that
charity which was in the primitive church: and for this purpose did Saint
Benet seek a solitary life, and then after him Barnarde, and after that divers
other did associate themselves together, for this intent only that they might use
the pure and simple life of christian men. after in process of time when their
riches and ceremonies did increase, their true godliness and simpleness did
abate and decrease. And now although we see men of religion to be overmuch
out of good order, and to use manners like unto gentiles, yet is the world filled
with new institutions and kinds of religion as though they should not fall to
the same point hereafter that other have done afore them. In times past, as I
said, a religious life was nothing but a solitary life. now these be called religious
which be altogether drowned in worldly business, using plainly certain tyranny
in worldly matters, and yet these for their apparel and title I cannot tell what,
doth challenge such holiness to their selves that they do account all other in
comparison of themselves no christian men at all. Why do we make so strait
and narrow Christ's religion which he would have so large? we be moved with
magnifical and high terms, I pray you what thing else is a city but a great
monastery? Monks be obedient to their abbot and governour, the citizens obey
the bishops and curates, whom Christ himself made rulers, and not the authority of man. monks live in idleness, and be fed of other men's liberality, pos-
sessing that amongst them in common, which they never laboured or sweat for
(yet speak I nothing of them that be vicious). The citizens bestow that which
they have gotten with their labour and great travail, to them that have need,

every man as he is of ability and power. Now as concerning the vow of chastity I dare not be bold to express what difference is betwixt the religious man unmarried and the chaste matrimony of the other. And to be short he shall not very greatly lack those three vows of man's invention, that doth keep and observe purely and sincerely that first only vow which we all solemnly make unto Christ, and not unto man, when we receive our baptism. And if we compare those that be evil of one kind, with those that be evil of the other, without doubt the temporal men be much better. But if we compare those which be good of the one sort with those that be good of the other there is little difference, if there be any at all, saving that those appear to be more religious that keep their religion and duty with less coercion. rest is therefore that no man foolishly stand in his own conceit, neither for his diversity of living from other men, nor despise or condemn the rule or order of other men's living. But in every kind of living let this be our common study, that every man according to his power endeavour himself to attain unto the mark of Christ, which is set open to all men, and that every man do exhort other to it, and also help other, neither envying them that over run us in this course, nor disdaining them that be weak and cannot yet overtake us. conclusion when every man hath done that he can, let him not be like unto the Pharisey whom the Gospel maketh mention of, which doth boast his good deeds unto God saying: I fast twice in the week, I pay all my tithes and so forth. But after Christ's counsel let him speak from the heart and to himself, and not to other, saying I am an unprofitable servant, for I have done no more than I ought to do. There is no man that better trusteth than he that so distrusteth. There is no man further from true religion than he that thinketh himself to be very religious. Nor Christ's godliness is never at worse point than when that thing which is worldly is writhen unto Christ, and the authority of man is preferred unto the authority of God. We must all hang of that head if we will be true christian men. Moreover whosoever is obedient to a man which doth persuade and call him unto Christ, he is obedient unto Christ, and not unto man. Whosoever doth tolerate and suffer those men which be subtle, cruel and imperious, teaching that thing which maketh not for religion, but for their tyranny, he useth the patience meet for a christian man, so that these things which they command be not utterly wicked and contrary to Christ's doctrine, for then it shall be convenient to have that answer of the apostles at hand: we must rather be obedient unto God than to any man.

But we have long ago passed the measure and quantity of an epistle, so greatly the time deceiveth us, whiles we come and talk most pleasantly with our well-beloved friend. This book is sent unto you in Frobenius' print, as though it were new-born again, much more ornate and better corrected than it was before. I have put unto it certain fragments of mine old study in times past. Methought it most convenient to dedicate this edition (such as it is) unto you, that whosoever shall take any precepts to live well of Erasmus, should have an example ready at hand of our father Wolzius. Our Lord preserve you, good father, the honour and worship of all religion. I pray you counsel Sapidus that he be wise, that is, that he go forth as he hath begun: and to Wynphelyngus ye shall speak also, that he prepare all his armour to fight shortly with the Turks, forasmuch as he hath kept war long enough with keepers of concubines. And I have great hope and trust to see him once a bishop, and to ride upon a mule, and to be set high in honour with a mitre and cross. But in earnest I pray you commend me heartily both unto them and unto Ruferus and the rest of my friends, and in your devout prayers made to God I pray you remember Erasmus, and pray for his soul's health. At Basyle the even of the assumption of our Lady, in the year of our Lord God M. CCCCC. and xviii.

A COMPENDIOUS TREATISE OF THE SOLDIER OF CHRIST, CALLED ENCHIRIDION, WHICH ERASMUS OF ROTERDAME WROTE UNTO A CERTAIN COURTIER, A FRIEND OF HIS.

THOU hast desired me with fervent study, singular beloved brother in Christ, that I should describe for thee compendiously, a certain craft of virtuous living, by whose help thou mightest attain a virtuous mind, according to a true christian man. For thou sayest that thou art and hast been a great while weary of the pastime of the court. dost compass in thy mind by what means thou mightest escape Egypt with all her both vices and pleasures, and be prepared happily with the captain Moses unto the journey of virtue. more I love thee, the gladder I am of this thine so holy purpose, which I trust (yea without our help) he that hath vouchsafed to stir it up in thee, shall make prosperous, and bring to good effect. Notwithstanding yet have I very gladly and willingly accomplished thy desire, partly because thou art so great a friend of mine, partly also because thou requirest so charitable things. Now enforce thyself, and do thine endeavour, that neither thou mayst seem to have desired my service and duty in vain, or else I to have satisfied my mind without any fruit. Yea let us both indifferently beseech the benign spirit of Jesu, that he both put wholesome things in my mind while I write and make the same to thee of strength and efficacy.

We must watch and look about us evermore while we be in this life

CHAPTER I

THE first point is, we must needs have in mind continually, that the life of mortal men is nothing but a certain perpetual exercise of war: as Job witnesseth, a warrior proved to the uttermost and never overcome. that the most part of men be overmuch deceived, whose minds this world as a juggler holdeth occupied with delicious and flattering pleasures, which also as though they had conquered all their enemies, make holiday out of season, none otherwise verily than in a very assured peace. is a marvellous thing to behold how without care and circumspection we live, how idly we sleep, now upon the one side, and now upon the other, when without ceasing we are besieged with so great a number of armed vices, sought and hunted for with so great craft, invaded daily with so great lying await. over thy head wicked devils that never sleep, but keep watch for our destruction, armed against us with a thousand deceits, with a thousand crafts of noysances, which enforce from on high to wound our minds with weapons burning and dipped in deadly poison, than the which weapons neither Hercules nor Cephalus had ever a surer dart, except they be received on the sure and impenetrable shield of faith. again, on the right hand and on the left hand, afore and behind, this world striveth against us, which after the saying of Saint John is set all on vice and mischief: and therefore to Christ both contrary and hated. Neither is it one manner of fight, for sometime with groans of adversity raging, as with open war he shaketh the walls of the soul. Sometime with great promises (but yet most vain) he provoketh to treason: and sometime by undermining he stealeth on us unaware to catch us among the idle and careless men. of all underneath, the slippery serpent, the first breaker of peace, father of unquietness, otherwhiles hid in the green grass, lurking in his caves, wrapped together in a hundred round coils ceaseth not to watch and lie in wait beneath in the heel of woman, whom he once poisoned. the woman is understood the carnal part of a man, otherwise called sensuality.

This is our Eve by whom the most crafty serpent doth entice and draw our minds to mortal and deadly pleasures. And furthermore as though it were but a trifle that so great a company of enemies should assault us on every side, we bear about with us wheresoever we go in the very secret parts of the mind an enemy nearer than one of acquaintance, or one of household. And as nothing is more inward, so nothing is more perilous. is the old and earthly Adam, which, by acquaintance and customary familiarity, is more near to us than a citizen, and is in all manner studies and pastimes to us more contrary than any mortal enemy, whom thou canst keep off with no bulwark, neither is it lawful to expel him out of thy pavilion. This fellow must be watched with an hundred eyes, lest peradventure he setteth open the castle or city of God for devils to enter in. Seeing therefore that we be vexed with so fearful and cruel war, and that we have to do or strive with so many enemies, which have conspired and sworn our death, which be so busy, so appointed, so false and expert: ought not we madmen on the other side to arm ourselves and take weapons in our hands to keep watch and have all things suspect? But we as though all things were at rest and peace, sleep so fast that we rowte again and give ourself to idleness, to pleasure, and as the common proverb is, give our minds to revelling and making good cheer, as though our life were a feasting or banqueting, such as the Greeks used, and not warfare. For in the stead of tents and pavilions we tumble and welter in our beds. And in the stead of sallettes and hard armour we be crowned with roses and fresh flowers, bathed in damask and rose waters, smoked in pomanders and with musk balls, changing points of war with riot and idleness. And in the stead of weapons belonging to the war, we handle and take unto us the unhardy harp, as this peace were not of all wars the most shameful. For whosoever is at one with vices, hath broken truce made between him and God in time of baptism. And thou, oh madman, criest peace, peace, when thou hast God thine enemy, which only is peace and the author of peace, and he himself with open mouth crieth the contrary by the mouth of his prophet, there is no peace to sinners or wicked persons which love not God. And there is none other condition of peace with him except that we (as long as we war in the fortress of this body) with deadly hate and with all our might hold fight against vices. For if we be at one with them, we shall have him twice our enemy, which only being our friend may make us blessed. And if he be our foe may destroy us, both because that we stand on their side which only can never agree with God, for how can light and darkness agree? and also that because we as men most unkind abide not by the promise that we made to him, but unjustly have broken the appointment made between him and us with protestation and holy ceremonies. thou christian man, rememberest thou not when thou wert professed and consecrate with the holy mysteries of the fountain of life, how thou boundest thyself to be a faithful soldier unto thy captain Christ, to whom thou owest thy life twice, both because he gave it thee, and also because he restored it again to thee, to whom thou owest more than thou art able to pay? Cometh it not to thy mind how when thou were bound with his sacraments as with holy gifts, thou were sworn with words for the nonce to take the part of so courteous an emperoure, and that thou didst curse and ban thine own head, desiring vengeance to fall upon thine own self, if thou didst not abide by thy promise? what intent was the sign of the cross printed in thy forehead, but that as long as thou livest thou shouldst fight under his standard? For what intent wert thou anointed with his holy oil, but that thou for ever shouldst wrestle and fight against vices? What shame and how great abomination is it accounted with all men if a man forsake his king or chief lord? Why settest thou so light, then, by thy captain Christ? neither kept down with the fear of him, seeing he is God, nor refraining for love, seeing for thy sake he was made man, and seeing thou usurpest his name thou ought to remember what thou hast promised him. Why departest thou away from him like a false forsworn man, and goest unto thine enemy, from whence he once redeemed thee with the ransom of his precious blood? Why dost thou, so oft a renegate, war and fight under the standard of his adversary? With what face presumest thou to set up contrary banners against thy king which for thy sake bestowed his own life? Whosoever is not on his part, as he saith himself (Luke 11) standeth against him. And he that gathereth not with him scattereth abroad. Thou warrest not only with filthy title or quarrel, but also for a miserable reward. Wilt thou hear whosoever thou be that art servant or soldier to the world, what shall be thy meed? Paul the standard-bearer in the war of Christ, answereth thee. reward (saith he) of sin is death. And who would take upon him to fight in a just and an honest cause, if he were sure to die but bodily only, and thou fightest in a wrong and also a filthy quarrel to obtain for thy reward the death of thy soul. In these mad wars that man maketh against man, either through beastly fury or for miserable necessity: seest thou not if at any time the greatness of the prey promised or hoped for, or comfort of the captain, or the cruelness of the enemies, or shame of cowardice cast in their teeth, or in conclusion if desire of praise hath pricked and stirred up the soldiers' minds: with what courage and with what lusty stomachs finish they whatsoever labour remaineth, how little they regard their lives, with how great fierceness run they upon their enemies, well is him that may go foremost. I beseech thee, how small is the reward which those wretched men go about to get with so great jeopardies and diligence? Verily but to have praise of a wretched man their captain, and that they might be praised with a rude and homely song, such as are used to be made in the time of war, to have haply their names written in a harper's beadroll, to get a garland of grass or oaken leaves, or at the most to bring home a little more vantage or winning with them. We, on the other side clean contrary, be kindled neither with shame nor with hope of reward, and yet he beholdeth us while we fight that shall quit our pain if we win the field. But what reward setteth forth the chief ruler of our game for them that win the mastery? not mules as Achilles did in Homer, not tripods, that is to say meat boards with three feet, as Eneas did in Virgil: but such as the eye never saw, nor the ear never heard, neither could sink into the heart of man. And these rewards he giveth in the mean season to his (whiles they be yet fighting) as solaces and things to comfort them in their labours and travails. And what hereafter? Certes, blessed immortality. But in games of sport, as running, wrestling, leaping, in which the chiefest part of reward is praise, they which be overcome have likewise their rewards assigned unto them. But our matter is tried with great and doubtful peril, neither we fight for praise, but for life, and as reward of most value is proffered to him that quitteth himself most manfully, so pain most terrible is appointed for him that giveth back. Heaven is promised to him that fighteth lustily. And why is not the quick courage of a gentle stomach enflamed with the hope of so blessed a reward, namely what He promiseth, which as he cannot die, even so he cannot deceive? things be done in the sight of God which all things beholdeth. We have all the company of Heaven beholders of our conflict. And how are we not moved, at the least way, even for very shame? He shall praise our virtue and diligence, of whom to be lauded is very felicity. Why seek we not this praise, yea, with the loss of our lives? It is a cowardly mind that will be quickened with no manner of reward. The veriest heartless coward in the world for fear of perils ofttime taketh courage to him. And in worldly battles though thine adversary be never so cruel, yet rageth he but on thy goods and body only. more than that could cruel Achilles do to Hector? But here the immortal part of thee is assaulted and thy carcass is not drawn about the sepulchre as Hector's, but thy body and soul is cast down into hell: there the greatest calamity or hurt is, that a sword shall separate the soul from the body: here is taken from thy soul the life, which is God himself. It is natural for the body to die, which if no man kill, yet must it needs die. But thy soul to die, is extreme misery. how great cawtell avoid we the wounds of the body, with how great diligence cure we them, and set we so little of the wounds of the soul. Our hearts ariseth and grudgeth at the remembrance of death of the body as a terrible or outrageous thing, because it is seen with bodily eyes. The soul to die, because no man seeth and few believeth, therefore very few fear it. And is this death more cruel yet than the other? Even as much as the soul doth pass the body, and God excelleth the soul. Wilt thou that I show thee certain conjectures, examples or tokens whereby thou mayest perceive the sickness and death of the soul? stomach digesteth ill, it keepeth no meat, thou perceivest by and by thy body to be out of temper. And bread is not so natural meat to the body as the word of God is meat for thy soul. If that seem bitter, if thy mind rise against it, why doubtest thou yet but that the mouth of the soul is out of taste, and infected with some disease? If thy memory the stomach of the soul, keep not the learning of God, if by continual meditation thou digestest not, if when it is digested, thou sendest it not to all parts by operation, thou hast an evident token that thy soul is acrased. When thy knees for weakness bow under thee, and it be much work to draw thy limbs after thee, thou perceivest plainly thy body to be evil at ease. And dost thou not perceive the sickness of thy soul, when he grudgeth and is weak and faint to all deeds of piety, when he hath no strength to suffer patiently the least rebuke in the world, and is troubled and angry with the loss of a halfpenny? after that the sight is departed from the eyes, and the ears cease to hear, after that all the body hath lost his feeling: no man doubteth then but the soul is departed. When the eyes of the heart be waxen dim, insomuch that thou canst not see the most clearest light, which is virtue or truth: when thou hearest not with thy inward ears the voice of God: when thou lackest all thy inward feeling and perceiving of the knowledge of God, thinkest thou that thy soul is alive? Thou seest thy brother ungoodly entreated, thy mind is nothing moved, so thy matter be in good case. Why feeleth thy soul nothing here? Certainly because he is dead. Why dead? Because her life is away, that is God. verily, where God is, there is charity, love and compassion of thy neighbours, for God is that charity. For if thou were a quick member, how could any part of thy body ache, thou not sorrowing, no not once feeling or perceiving it? Take a more evident token. hast deceived thy friend, thou hast committed adultery, thy soul hath caught a deadly wound, and yet it grieveth thee not, insomuch as thou joyest as it were of great winning, and boastest thyself of that thou shamefully hast committed. Believe surely that thy soul lieth dead. Thy body is not alive if it feel not the pricking of a pin. And is thy soul alive which lacketh the feeling of so great a wound? Thou hearest some man use lewd and presumptuous communication, words of backbiting, unchaste and filthy, raging furiously against his neighbour: think not the soul of that man to be alive. There lieth a rotten carcase in the sepulchre of that stomach from whence such stench ariseth and infecteth every man that cometh nigh. Christ called the Pharisees painted sepulchres. Why so?

Because they bear dead souls about with them. And king David the prophet saith, their throat is a sepulchre wide open, they spake deceitfully with their tongues. bodies of holy people be the temples of the Holy Ghost. And lewd men's bodies be the sepulchre of dead corpses, that the interpretations of the grammarians to them might well be applied, Soma quasi Sima. is called a body because it is the burial, that is to say, the grave of the soul. The breast is the sepulchre, the mouth and the throat is the gaping of the sepulchre, and the body destitute of the soul is not so dead as is the soul when she is forsaken of Almighty God, neither any corpse stinketh in the nose of man so sore as the stench of a soul buried four days offendeth the nose of God and all saints. Therefore conclude, whensoever dead words proceed out of thy heart, it must needs be that a dead corpse lieth buried within. For when (according to the Gospel) the mouth speaketh of the abundance of the heart, no doubt he would speak the lively words of God, if there were life present, that is to wit, God. In another place of the Gospel the disciples say to Christ, Master, whither shall we go, thou hast the words of life? Why so, I pray thee, the words of life? Certainly for because they sprung out of the soul from whom the Godhead, which restored us again to life immortal, never departed not yet one moment. The physician easeth the body sometimes when thou art diseased. Good and holy men sometimes have called the body dead to life again. But a dead soul nothing but God only of his free and singular power restoreth to life again, yea, and he restoreth her not again if she being dead have once forsaken the body. Moreover of the bodily death is the feeling little or none at all. But of the soul, is the feeling eternal. And though also the soul in that case be more than dead, yet as touching the feeling of eternal death, she is ever immortal. Therefore seeing we must needs fight with so strange and marvellous jeopardy, what dulness, what negligence, what foolishness is that of our mind, whom fear of so great mischief sharpeneth not. again on the contrary part there is no cause wherefore either the greatness of peril, or else the multitude, the violence, the subtlety of thine adversaries should abate the courage of thy mind. It cometh to thy mind how grievous an adversary thou hast. Remember also on the other side how present how ready at hand thou hast help and succour. Against thee be innumerable, yea but he that taketh thy part, himself alone is more of power than all they. If God be on our side, what matter is it who be against us? If he stay thee, who shall cast thee down? But thou must be inflamed in all thy heart and brain in fervent desire of victory. it come to thy remembrance that thou strivest not, nor hast not to do with a fresh soldier and a new adversary, but with him that was many years ago discomforted, overthrown, spoiled and led captive in triumph of us, but then in Christ our head, by whose might no doubt he shall be subdued again in us also. Take heed therefore that thou be a member of the body and thou shalt be able to do all things in the power of the head. thyself thou art very weak, in him thou art valiant, and nothing is there that thou art not able to do. Wherefore the end of our war is not doubtful, because the victory dependeth not of fortune, but is put wholly in the hands of God, and by him in our hands. No man is here that hath not overcome, but he that would not. The benignity of our protector never failed man. If thou take heed to answer and to do thy part again, thou art sure of the victory, for he shall fight for thee, and his liberality shall be imputed to thee for merit. Thou must thank him altogether for the victory, which first of all himself alone being immaculate, pure and clean from sin, oppressed the tyranny of sin. But this victory shall not come without thine own diligence also, for he that said, Have confidence, I have overcome the world, would have thee to be of a good comfort, but not careless and negligent. On this manner in conclusion is his strength, and by him we shall overcome. by his example, we shall fight as he fought, wherefore thou must so keep a mean course, as it were between Scylla and Charibdis, that neither trusting too much and bearing thee overbold upon the grace of God thou be careless and reckless, neither yet so mistrusting in thyself, feared with the difficulties of the war, do cast from thee courage, boldness, or confidence of mind together with harness and weapons also.

Of the weapons to be used in the war of a Christian man

CHAPTER II

AND I suppose that nothing pertaineth so much to the discipline of this war than that thou surely know, and presently have recorded and exercised in thy mind alway with what kind of armour or weapons thou oughtest to fight, and against what enemies thou must encounter and joust. Moreover that thy weapons be always ready at hand, lest thine so subtle an enemy should take thee sleeping and unarmed. In these worldly wars a man may be oftentimes at rest, as in the deep of the winter, or in time of truce: but we as long as we keep war in this body, may depart from our harness and weapons no season, no not as the saying is one finger breadth. must ever stand afore the tents and make watch, for our adversary is never idle: but when he is most calm and still, when he feigneth to flee or to make truce, even then most of all he imagineth guile: and thou hast never more heed to keep watch than when he maketh countenance or semblance of peace. Thou hast never less need to fear than when he assaulteth thee with open war. Therefore let thy first care be that thy mind be not unarmed. We arm our body, because we would have no need to fear the dagger or privy murderer of the thief. Shall we not arm our mind likewise, that he might be in safeguard? Our enemies be armed to destroy us, doth it grieve us to take our weapons of defence, that we perish not? They watch to kill, shall not we watch to be out of danger? But of the armour and weapons of a christian man we shall make special mention when we come to the places convenient. the mean season to speak briefly, whosoever will assail with battle the seven nations that be called Cananei, Cethei, Amorrei, Pherezei, Gergezei, Evei, and Jebuzei, that is to say, whosoever will take upon him to fight against the whole host of vices, of the which seven be counted as chief captains, must provide him of two special weapons. and knowledge, otherwise called learning. Paul would we should be ever armed, which biddeth us pray continually without stop. Prayer pure and perfect lifteth up thine affection to heaven, a tower beyond thine enemies' reach. Learning or knowledge fenceth or armeth the mind with wholesome precepts and honest opinions, and putteth thee ever in remembrance of virtue, so that neither can be lacking to the other. These twain cleaveth so together like friends, the one ever requiring the other's help. The one maketh intercession and prayeth. The other sheweth what is to be desired and what thou oughtest to pray. To pray fervently, and (as James exhorteth us) without doubting or mistrusting, faith and hope bringeth to pass. To pray in the name of Jesu, which is nothing else but to desire things wholesome for thy soul's health only, learning or doctrine teacheth thee. not Christ to the sons of Zebedei, Ye know not what ye ask? But prayer verily is the more excellent, as she that cometh and talketh familiarly with Almighty God. Yet for all that is doctrine no less necessary. And I cannot tell whether that thou, fled from Egypt, mightest without great jeopardy commit thyself to so long a journey, so hard and full of difficulty, without the captains Aaron and Moses. which was charged with things dedicate to the service of God's temple, betokeneth prayer. By Moses is figured the knowledge of the law of God. And as knowledge of God ought not to be unprofitable, so prayer should not be faint, slack, without courage or quickness. Moses with the weapons of prayer fought against his enemies, but had his hands lifted up to Heaven, which when he let down, the Israelites had the worse. Thou, haply, when thou prayest, considerest only how much of thy psalms thou hast mumbled up, and thinkest much babbling to be the strength and virtue of prayer: which is chiefly the vice of them which (as infants) cleave to the literal sense, and are not yet grown up to the ripeness of the spirit. But hear what Christ teacheth us in Matthew, saying, When ye pray speak not much, as the ethnics and gentiles do, for they think their prayers to be accepted because of much babbling. Counterfeit them not therefore, for your Father knoweth whereof ye have need before ye desire it of Him. And Paul to the Corynthes despiseth ten thousand words babbled with mouth in comparison of five spoken in knowledge. Moses opened not his lips, and yet God said to him, Why criest thou so to me? It is not the noise of thy lips, but the fervent desire of thy mind, which (as it were a very shrill voice) beateth the ears of God. Let this, therefore, be a customable thing with thee that as soon as thine enemy ariseth against thee, and the vices which thou hast forsaken trouble thee, thou then without tarrying with sure confidence and trust lift up thy mind to heaven, whence help shall come to thee, and thither also lift up thy hands. The surest thing of all is to be occupied in deeds of piety, that thy deeds may be referred and applied, not to worldly business but unto Christ. Yet lest thou shouldst despise the help of knowledge, consider one thing. Beforetime it was enough for the Israelites to flee and escape from their enemies, but they were never so bold as to provoke the Amalachytes, and to try with them hand for hand before they were refreshed with manna from heaven and water running out of the hard rock. noble warrior David refreshed and made strong with these cates, set nought by the whole host of his adversaries, saying, Oh good Lord thou hast set a table of meat before me to defend me against all men that trouble me. Believe me well, brother singularly beloved in my heart, there is none so great violence of thy foes, that is to say, none so great temptation which fervent study or meditation of holy scripture is not able to put aback, nor any so grievous adversity which it maketh not easy. And lest I should seem to be somewhat too bold an interpreter (though I could defend myself with great authority) what thing, I pray thee, could more properly have signified the knowledge of the secret law of God than did manna? For first in that it sprang not out of the earth, but rained down from heaven. By this property thou perceivest the difference between the doctrine of God and the doctrine of man. For all holy scripture came by divine inspiration and from God the author. In that it is small or little in quantity, is signified the humility, lowliness or homeliness of the style under rude words including great mystery. That it is white, by this property is signified the purity and cleanness of God's law. For there is no doctrine of man which is not defiled with some black spot of error, only the doctrine of Christ everywhere bright, everywhere pure and clean. That it is somewhat hard and some deal rough and sharp, betokeneth secret mysteries hid in the literal sense. If thou handle the outer side and if I may so call it the cod, what is more hard or unsavoury? They tasted but the outer rind of manna which said to Christ, This is a hard saying, and who may abide the hearing thereof. But get out the spiritual sense, and nothing is more sweeter nor more full of pleasure and sweet juice. Moreover manna is in the Hebrew tongue as much to say as What is this? Which question agreeth well to holy scripture, which hath nothing in it idle or in vain, no not one tittle or prick, unworthy to be searched, unworthy to be pondered, unworthy of this saying, What is this? It is a common use unto the Holy Ghost to signify by water the knowledge of the law of God. Thou readest of the water of comfort by whose banks David rejoiceth to have been nourished up: thou readest of the waters which wisdom conveyeth into the tops of every way: thou readest of the mystical river into the which Ezechiel entered, and could not wade over: thou readest of the wells that Abraham digged, which when they were stopped of the Philistiens Isaac repaired again. Thou readest of twelve fountains in which the Israelytes after they had walked through forty mansions, and began then to be weary and faint, rested and refreshed themselves and made them strong to the long journey of desert.

Thou also readest in the Gospel of the well whereupon Christ sat wearied in his journey. readest of the water of Siloe, whither he sendeth the blind to recover his sight. Thou readest of the water poured into the basin to wash the apostles' feet. And because it needeth not to rehearse all places in this signification, often mention is made in scripture of wells, fountains and rivers, by which is signified nothing else but that we ought to enquire and search diligently for the mysteries hid in scripture. What signifieth water hid in the veins of the earth but mystery covered or hid in the literal sense? What meaneth the same conveyed abroad but mystery opened and expounded? Which being spread and dilated both wide and broad to the edifying of the hearers, what cause is there why it might not be called a river? Wherefore if thou dedicate thyself wholly to the study of scripture and exercise thy mind day and night in the law of God, no fear shall trouble thee, neither by day nor night: but thou shalt against all assaults of thine enemies be armed and exercised also. And I disallow it not utterly if a man for a season (to begin withal) do exercise and sport himself in works of poets and philosophers which were gentiles, as in his A B C or introductory to a more perfect thing, so that he taste of them measurably, and whiles youth shall give him leave, and even as though a man took them in his way, but not abide and tarry upon them still, and to wax old and die in them, as he were bound to the rocks of Sirenes, is to put his whole delectation in them and never go farther. For holy Basilius to such pastime exhorteth young men, whom he himself had induced to the conversation of christian men. And our Augustyn calleth back again his friend Licentius to pass the time with the Muses, neither Jerom repenteth himself that he hath loved a woman taken prisoner in war. Cyprian is commended because he garnished the temple of God with the spoils of the Egyptians. But in no case would I that thou with the gentiles' learning shouldest also suck the gentiles' vices and conversation. For if thou do not, thou shalt find many things helping to honest living, neither is it to be refused whatsoever an author (yea though he be a gentile) teacheth well. For Moses verily though he were never so familiar with God, yet despised he not the counsels of his father-in-law Jetro. Those sciences fashion and quicken a child's wit, and maketh him apt aforehand marvellously to the understanding of holy scripture. Whereunto suddenly and irreverently to presume with hands and feet unwashed, is in manner a certain kind of sacrilege. And Jerom checketh the shameless pertness of them which straightway from secular or worldly science dare take in hand to meddle or interpret holy scripture. But how much shamefuller do they which never tasted other science, and yet at the first dare do the same thing. But as the scripture is not much fruitful if thou stand and stick still in the letter: in like manner the poetry of Homer and Virgil shall not profit a little, if thou remember that it must be understood in the sense allegory, which thing no man will deny that hath assayed or tasted of the learning of old antiquities never so little, yea with the tip of his tongue, or uttermost part of his lips. As for the poets which write uncleanly, I would counsel thee not once to touch them, or at the least way not to look far in them: except thou can the better abhor vices when they be described to thee, and in comparisons of filthy things the more fervently love things honest. Of the philosophers my mind is that thou follow them that were of Plato's sect, because both in very many sentences, and much more in their style and manner speaking, they come very nigh to the figure and property of speech used of the prophets and in the Gospels. And to make an end shortly, it shall be profitable to taste of all manner of learning of the gentiles, if it so be done as I shewed before, both in years according and measurably, moreover with caution and judgment discreetly, furthermore with speed and after the manner of a man that intendeth but to pass over the country only and not to dwell or inhabit, in conclusion (which thing is chiefest of all) if everything be applied and referred to Christ. For so all shall be clean to them that be clean when on the other side to them that be unclean nothing is clean. it shall be no rebuke to thee, if after the example of Salomon thou nourish up at home in thy house sixty queens, eighty sovereign ladies and damsels innumerable of secular wisdom: so that the wisdom of God be above all other, thy best beloved, thy dove, thy sweetheart, which only seemeth beautiful. And an Israelyte loveth a stranger and a barbarous damsel, overcome with her beauty: but first he shaveth off her hair and pareth her nails, and maketh her of an alien an Israelyte. And the prophet Ozee married an harlot, and of her had children not for himself, but for the Lord of Sabaoth and the holy fornication of the prophet augmented the household of God. Hebrews after they had forsaken Egypt lived with light and pure white bread for a season, but it was not sufficient to so great a journey. Therefore that bread loathed at once, thou must make as good speed as can be unto manna of celestial wisdom the which shall nourish thee abundantly and strengthen thee until thou obtain thy purpose, and win by victory the reward that never shall cease: but thou must ever remember in the mean season that holy scripture may not be touched but with clean and washen hands, that is to understand, but with high pureness of mind, lest that which of itself is a preservative or treacle, by thine own fault turn to thee into poison, lest manna to thee begin to putrify, except that thou convey or send it into the inward parts of thy mind and affection, and lest haply it should fortune to thee as it did to Oza, which feared not to set his profane and unclean hands to the ark of God inclining on the one side and with sudden death was

punished for his lewd service. The first point is that thou have good opinion of
the holy scriptures, that thou esteem them of no less value and dignity than
they are worthy to be esteemed, and that they came out of the secret closet of
the mind of God. Thou shalt perceive that thou art inspired of God moved
inwardly, rapt and in an unspeakable manner altered and changed to another
manner, figure or shape, if thou shalt come religiously, if with reverence and
meekly thou shalt see the pleasures, delicacies, or dainties of the blessed spouse.
Thou shalt see the precious jewels of rich Salomon, thou shalt see the secret
treasure of eternal wisdom: but beware that thou break not malapertly into the
secret closet, the door is low, beware lest thou strike the door with thy head,
and be fain to leap back again. Think on this wise, nothing that thou seest
with thine eyes, nothing that thou handlest with thy fingers to be indeed the
same thing which it appeareth, so surely as these things be true in holy scripture: that if heaven and earth should perish, yet of the words of God not one
jot or tittle shall perish, but all shall be fulfilled. Though men lie, though men
err, yet the verity of God neither deceiveth nor is deceived. the interpreters of
scripture, choose them above all other that go farthest from the letter, which
chiefly next after Paul be Origene, Ambrose, Jerom and Augustyne. For I see
the divines of later time stick very much in the letter, and with good will give
more study to subtle and deceitful arguments, than to search out the mysteries,
as though Paul had not said truly our law to be spiritual. I have heard some
men myself which stood so greatly in their own conceit with the fantastical
traditions, imaginations and inventions of man, that they despised the interpretation of old doctors that were nigh to Christ and his apostles both in time
and living also, and account them as dreams, and Master Dunce gave them
such confidence that notwithstanding they never once read the holy scripture,
yet thought they themselves to be perfect divines, which persons though they
speak things never so crafty and subtle, yet whether they speak things worthy
of the Holy Ghost and the meek spirit of Christ or not, let other men judge.
But if thou haddest liefer to be somewhat lusty and quick of spirit, than to be
armed to contention, that is to say to brawling or scolding: if thou seek rather
to have thy soul made fat, than thy wit to be vainly delighted: study and read
over chiefly the old doctors and expositors, whose godliness and holy life is
more proved and known, whose religion to God is more to be pondered and
looked upon, whose learning is more plenteous and sage also, whose style is
neither bare nor rude and interpretation more agreeable to the holy mysteries.
And I say not this because I despise these new divines, but because I set more
by things more profitable and more apt for the purpose. also the Spirit of God
hath a certain tongue or speech appropriate to himself, he hath his figures

similitudes, parables, comparisons, proverbs and riddles which thou must observe and mark diligently, if thou wouldest understand them. The wisdom of God stuttereth and lispeth as it were a diligent mother fashioneth her words according to our infancy and feebleness. She giveth milk to them that be infants in Christ, weak meat to feeble stomachs. Thou therefore make speed thou were a man, make haste to perfect and strong meat, and prepare a man's stomach. She stoopeth down and boweth herself to thy humility and lowness. Arise then upon the other side and ascend to her height and excellency. It is like a monster and unnatural to be ever a child. He is too heartless that never ceaseth to be feeble and weak. The recording of one verse shall be more savoury in thy mouth, and shall nourish thee better if thou break the cod and taste of the sweetness which is within, than if thou shouldest sing the whole psalter, d only after the literal sense, whereof verily I give admonition a great deal the rather, because I know by experience that this error hath not infected the lay people only, but also the minds of them which profess and shew outward in their habit and name or title, perfect religion, insomuch that they think the very service of God to be put chiefly in this one thing, if they shall say over every day as much as they can of the psalms scarce understood, yea, in the literal sense. I think any other thing to be the cause why we see the charitable living of our monks and cloisterers to fail everywhere, to be so cold, so slacked, so faint and so to vanish away, but that they continue all their, life and wax old in the letter and never enforce to come to the spiritual knowledge of scripture, neither hear they Christ crying in the Gospel, the flesh, that is to say, the letter, or that ye see outward profiteth not at all. It is the Spirit within that quickeneth or giveth life. hear not Paul affirming with his master, that the letter killeth, and it is the spirit giveth life. And again we know (saith he) that the law is spiritual, and not carnal. Spiritual things must be compared with spiritual things. time past the Father of all spiritual gifts would be honoured in the mountain, but now he will be honoured in the spirit. Howbeit I despise not the feebleness of them, which for lack of knowledge and understanding doth that they only be able to do, pronouncing the mystical psalms with pure faith without dissimulation or hypocrisy, rather as in charms and enchantments of magic certain words not understood, no not of them which pronounce them, yet be believed to be of virtue and strength. Even so the words of God, though they be not perfectly understood, nevertheless we must trust that they be profitable to them that either say them or hear them with perfect faith, with pure affection and mind, and that the angels which are present and doth understand be provoked to help them. And Paul despiseth not them which say psalms with their mouth which speaketh with tongues that thing they understand not: but he exhorteth them to leave their infancy, and to follow more perfect gifts, unto which if a man cannot attain, not through the default of a corrupt mind, but for lack of capacity, let him not bark against them which enforce better things. And after the precept of Paul let not him which eateth despise him which eateth not, neither he that eateth not judge him that eateth. Nevertheless I will not have thee which art endowed with so happy a wit to be slow and to tarry long in the barren letter, but to make speed unto more secret mysteries, and to help the continual endeavour and enforcement of thine industry and will with often prayers until he open to thee the book clasped with seven clasps, which hath the key of David, the which also shutteth and no man openeth the privities of the Father, which never man knew but his Son, and he to whom his Son hath vouchsafed to disclose them. But whither goeth our style aside? Mine intent was to describe the form of living not of learning: but I turned out of the way thus far while I laboured to shew thee a meet shop from whence thou oughtest to fetch thy new armour and weapons belonging to the new war. Therefore to come to our purpose again, if thou shalt pick and choose out of the books of the gentiles of every thing the best: and also if thou by the example of the bee, flying round about by the gardens of old authors shalt suck out only the wholesome and sweet juice (the poison refused and left behind) thy mind shall be better apparelled a great deal, and armed unto the common life or conversation, in which we live one with another in honest manner. For the philosophers and learned men of the gentiles in their war use certain weapons and armour not to be despised. Nevertheless whatsoever thing of honesty or truth thou findest anywhere, think that to be Christ's. that divine armour and (to speak as the poets do) that harness of Vulcanus' making, which with no weapons can be pierced, is fetched only out of the armoury of holy scripture, where our noble captain David laid up all his ordinance of war for his soldiers with which they should fight afar and at hand against the uncircumcised Philistiens. this harness was clothed neither Achilles, of whom Homer writeth, neither Eneas, of whom Virgil speaketh, though they be so feigned. Of which the one with ire, the other with love was overcome shamefully. And it is not spoken without reason that those weapons be not forged in the workhouse of man, but in the workhouse or forge that is common to Vulcan and Pallas, otherwise called Mynerva. poets the feigners of gods maketh Vulcan lord of fire, and Mynerva lady of wit, faculties, sciences and crafts, which thing I judge to be done in very deed (as thou mayest easily perceive) when the fire of love of God hath armed thy wit, endued with honest faculties so strongly, if all the world should fall on thy head yet should not the stroke put thee to fear. But first thou must cast away the harness of proud Saul, which rather loadeth a man than be anything necessary or profitable, and cumbered David ready to fight with Golyas and holpe him not at all. Moreover from the bank of the brook of holy scripture thou must gather five stones, which peradventure be the five words of Paul, which he speaketh in knowledge. Then take a sling in thy right hand; with these weapons is overthrown our only enemy, the father of pride, Sathan, whom at the last with what weapons did our head Christ Jesu overcome? Did not he smite the forehead of our adversary as it had been with stones fetched out of the brook when he answered him in time of temptation with words of scripture. thou hear the instruments or artillery of christian men's war? And the zeal of him (saith scripture) shall take harness and shall harness his creature to avenge his enemies, he will put on justice for his breastplate, and take for his helmet sure and true judgment. He will take a shield of equity impenetrable or that cannot be pierced, yea, and he will sharpen or fashion cruel wrath into a spear. Thou readest also in Isai he is armed with justice, as with an habergeon and a salet of health upon his head, he is clothed with the vestures of vengeance and covered as it were with a cloak of zeal. Now if thou list to go to the storehouse of Paul, that valiant captain, certainly thou shalt also find there the armour of war, not carnal things, but valiant in God to destroy fortresses and counsels, and every high thing that exalteth himself against the doctrine of God. Thou shalt find there the armour of God, by the which thou mayest resist in a woeful day. Thou shalt find the harness of justice on the right hand, and on the left thou shalt find the defence of thy sides' verity, and the habergeon of justice the buckler of faith, wherewith thou mayest quench all the hot and fiery weapons of thy cruel adversary. shalt find also the helmet of health and the sword of the Spirit, which is the word of God, with the which all if a man shall be diligently covered and fenced, he may boldly without fear bring forth the bold saying of Paul. Who shall separate us from the love of God? shall tribulation? shall straitness or difficulty? shall hunger? shall nakedness? shall peril? shall persecution? shall a sword? Behold how mighty enemies and how much feared of all men he setteth at nought. But hear also a certain greater thing, for it followeth. But in all things we have overcome by his help which loved us. And I am assured (saith he) that neither death, nor life, nor angels, neither principalities, neither virtues, neither present things, neither things to come, neither strength, neither height, neither lowness, nor none other creature shall or may separate us from the love of God which is in Christ Jesu. Oh happy trust and confidence which the weapons or armour of light giveth to Paul, that is by interpretation a little man, which calleth himself the refuse or outcast of the world! Of such armour therefore abundantly shall holy scripture minister to thee, if thou wilt occupy thy time in it with all thy might: so that thou shalt not need our counsel or admonitions. Nevertheless seeing it is thy mind, lest I should seem not to have obeyed thy request, I have forged for thee this little treatise called Enchiridion, that is to say, a certain little dagger, whom never lay out of thy hand, no not when thou art at meat or in thy chamber. Insomuch that if at any time thou shalt be compelled to make a pilgrimage in these worldly occupations, and shalt be too cumbered to bear about with thee the whole and complete armour and harness of holy scripture, yet commit not that the subtle lier in wait at any season should come upon thee and find thee utterly unarmed, but at the least let it not grieve thee to have with thee this little hanger, which shall not be heavy to bear, nor unprofitable for thy defence, for it is very little, yet if thou use it wisely, and couple with it the buckler of faith, thou shalt be able to withstand the fierce and raging assault of thine enemy: so that thou shalt have no deadly wound. But now it is time that I begin to give thee a certain rule of the use of these weapons which if thou shalt put in execution or practice, I trust it will come to pass that our captain Jesus Christ shall translate thee a conqueror out of this little castle or garrison into his great city Jerusalem with triumph, where is no rage at all of any battle, but eternal quietness, perfect peace, assured tranquillity: whereas in the mean season all hope and confidence of safeguard is put in armour and weapon.

That the first point of wisdom is to know thyself, and of
two manner wisdoms, the true wisdom, and the apparent

CHAPTER III

THAT excellent good thing desired and sought for of all men, is peace or
quietness: unto which the lovers of this world also refer all their study, but they
seek a false peace, and shoot at a wrong mark. The same peace the philosophers also promised unto the followers of their conclusions, but yet falsely, for
Christ only giveth it, the world giveth it not. come to this quietness the only
way or means is (if we make war) against ourself, if we fight strongly against
our own vices, for with these enemies God, is our peace, is at variance with
deadly hate, seeing he is naturally virtue itself and father and lord of all virtue.
And whereas a filthy puddle or a sink gathered together of all kind of vices, is
named of the stoics, are the most fervent defenders of virtue, foolishness, and
in our scripture the same is called malice, in like manner virtue or goodness
lacking in no point of both parts, is called wisdom. But after the saying of the
wise man—doth not wisdom overcome malice? The father and head of malice
is the ruler of darkness, Belial: whose steps whosoever followeth walketh in the
night and shall come to eternal night. On the other side the ground of wisdom
and indeed wisdom itself is Christ Jesus, which is very light and the brightness
of the glory of his Father, putting away by himself only the night of the foolishness of the world. The which (witnessing Paul) as he was made redemption
and justification to us that be born again in him: even likewise was made also
our wisdom. We (saith Paul) preach Christ crucified, which to the Jews is an
occasion of unity, and to the gentiles foolishness. But to the elected both of the
Jews and also of the gentiles we preach Christ the virtue or strength of God,
and the wisdom of God, by whose wisdom through his example we may beat
away the victory of our enemy malice, if we shall be wise in him in whom also
we shall be conquerors. much of this wisdom and take her in thine arms.
Worldly wisdom set at nought, which with false title and under a feigned

colour of honesty boasteth and showeth herself gay to fools, when after Paul there is no greater foolishness with God than worldly wisdom, thing that must be forgotten indeed again of him that will be wise indeed. any man (saith Paul) among you seemeth to be wise in this world, let him be a fool that he may be wise, for the wisdom of this world is foolishness with God. And a little afore Paul saith, It is written, I will destroy the wisdom of wise men, and the prudence of prudent men I will reprove. Where is the wise man, where is the subtle lawyer, where is the searcher of this world? Hath not God made the wisdom of this world foolishness? And I doubt not but even now with great hate these foolish wise men bark against thee, and these blind captains or guides of blind men cry out and roar against thee, saying that thou art deceived, thou dotest and art mad as a bedlam man, because thou intendest to depart unto Christward. These be in name only christian men, but in very deed they are both mockers and also enemies of Christ's doctrine. Take heed and beware that their foolish babbling move thee not, whose miserable blindness ought rather to be wept, sorrowed and mourned than to be counterfeited or followed. Oh what foolish kind of wisdom and clean out of order is this in trifles and things of no value, yea to filthiness only to be clear witted, ware and expert: but in those things which only make for our safe-guard or health, not to have much more understanding than a brute beast! Paul would we should be wise but in goodness, and children in evil. These men be wise to all iniquity: but they have no learning to do good. for as much as that fecund and Greek poet Hesiodus counteth him good for nothing which neither is wise of himself, neither yet will follow and do after him that giveth him good counsel: of what degree then shall they be counted which when they themselves be most shamefully deceived, yet never cease to trouble, to laugh to scorn and put in fear them which already be come to their wits again? But shall not the mocker be mocked? He that dwelleth in heaven shall mock them again, and our Lord shall laugh them to scorn. Thou readest in the Book of Sapience, They shall see verily and shall despise him, but God shall mock them. To be mocked of lewd men, is as it were a praise. And no doubt it is a blessed thing to follow our head, Christ and his apostles, and a fearful thing truly to be mocked of God. also (saith the Wisdom) will laugh when ye perish, and mock you when that thing hath happened to you which ye feared, that is to say, when they awaked out of their dream and come again to themselves, when it is too late, shall say, These be they whom we have had in derision and reproof, we for lack of understanding have counted their lives to be madness, and their end to be without honour. This wisdom is beastly, and as James saith, diabolic and of the devil, and is an enemy to God, whose end is destruction. always after this wisdom followeth as a waiting-servant or hand-maid mischievous presumption, after presumption followeth blindness of mind, after blindness of mind followeth fervent rage and tyranny of affections and appetites, after the tyranny of affections followeth the whole heap of all vices and liberty to do what he listeth. Then followeth custom, after followeth most wretched dulness or insensibility of mind, a dazing of the wits for lack of capacity. By which it is caused that evil men perceive not themselves to sin. And whiles they be in such insensibility without any feeling or perceiving of themselves, bodily death cometh suddenly on them, and after it followeth the second death, which is death everlasting. seest how the mother of the extreme mischief is worldly wisdom, but of the wisdom of Christ which the world thinketh foolishness, this wise thou readest. All good things came to men by heaps with her, and inestimable honesty by the hands of her. And I rejoiced in all things because this wisdom went before me, and I was not aware that she was mother of all good things. This wisdom bringeth with her as companions soberness and meekness. Meekness disposeth and maketh us apt to receive the spirit of God. For in the lowly, humble and meek person he rejoiceth to rest. And when the spirit hath replenished our minds with his sevenfold grace, then forth withal springeth that plenteous herbage of all virtue, with those blessed fruits of which the chief is the secret joy of a clear conscience, which joy is known of none but only of such to whom it hath chanced to taste of it. Joy that never vanisheth away, nor fadeth with the joys of this world, but increaseth and groweth to eternal gladness and mirth. This wisdom my brother (after the counsel of James) must thou require of God with fervent and burning desire. And after the counsel of the wise man dig her out of the veins of holy scripture, as it were treasure hid in the earth. The chief part of this wisdom is that thou shouldest know thyself, which word to have descended from heaven the antiquity believed, and so much hath that saying pleased great authors, that they judged all plenty of wisdom to be shortly comprehended in this little sentence, that is to wit, if a man know himself. But let the weight or authority of this conclusion and doctrine be of no value with us, except it agree with our learning. The mystical lover in Canticles threateneth his spouse, and biddeth her to get herself out of the doors, except she know herself, saying, O thou beautiful among all women, if thou know not thyself, go out of the doors and walk after the steps of thy flock and sort. Therefore let no man presumptuously take upon him this so great a thing, to think that he knoweth himself well enough. I am not sure whether any man knoweth his body unto the uttermost, and then how can a man know the state of his mind surely enough? Paul, whom God so loved that he saw the mysteries of the third heaven, yet durst he not judge himself which thing doubtless he would have been bold to do, if he had known himself surely enough. If so spiritual a man which discerneth all things, and is himself to be judged of no man, was not surely enough known to himself, how should we carnal men presume? In conclusion let him seem to be a very unprofitable soldier, which surely enough neither knew his own company, neither his enemies' host. so it is that one christian man hath not war with another but with himself, and verily a great host of adversaries spring out of our own flesh, out of the very bowels and inward part of us. Likewise as it is read in certain poets' tales of the brethren gendered of the earth. And there is so little difference between our enemy and our friend, and so hard to know the one from the other, that there is great jeopardy lest we somewhat recklessly or negligently defend our enemy instead of our friend, or hurt our friend instead of our enemy. The noble captain Josue was in doubt of an angel of light, saying Art thou on our part, or of our enemies' part. Therefore seeing that thou hast taken upon thee war against thyself, and the chief hope and comfort of victory is if thou know thyself to the uttermost, I will paint a certain image of thyself, as it were in a table, and set it before thine eyes that thou mayst perfectly know what thou art inwardly and within thy skin.

Of the outward and inward man

CHAPTER IV

A MAN is then a certain monstrous beast compact together of parts two or three of great diversity. a soul as of a certain goodly thing, and of a body as it were a brute or dumb beast. For certainly we so greatly excel not all other kinds of brute beasts in perfectness of body, but that we in all his natural gifts are found to them inferiors. In our minds verily we be so celestial and of godly capacity that we may surmount above the nature of angels, and be unite, knit and made one with God. If thy body had not been added to thee, thou hadst been a celestial or godly thing. this mind had not been grafted in thee, plainly thou hadst been a brute beast. two natures between themselves so diverse, that excellent workman had coupled together with blessed concord: but the serpent the enemy of peace put them asunder again with unhappy discord: so that now they neither can be separate without very great torment and pain, neither live joined together without continual war. plainly, after the common saying, each in the other holdeth the wolf by the ears, and either may say very well and accordingly to the other that proper and pleasant verse of Catullus, I neither can live with thee nor without thee. Such ruffling, wrangling and trouble they make between themselves with cumberous debate as things diverse, which indeed are but one. The body verily as he himself is visible, so delighteth he in things visible. As he is mortal, so followeth he things temporal. As he is heavy, so sinketh he downward. On the other part, the soul mindful of her celestial nature enforceth upward with great violence and with a terrible haste striveth and wrestleth with the heavy burden of the earthly body. She despiseth these things that are seen, for she knoweth them to be transitory, she seeketh true things of substance which be permanent and ever abiding, and because she is immortal and also celestial she loveth things immortal and celestial, and re-joiceth with things of like nature, except she be utterly drowned in the filth of the body and by contagiousness of him hath gone out of kind from her native gentleness. verily neither Prometheus, so much spoken of among poets, sowed this discord in us a portion of every beast mixed to our mind, neither our primitive and first making gave it, that is to say, it sprang not in us naturally, or nature gave it not to us in our first creation or nativity: but sin hath evil-corrupted and decayed that which was well created, sowing the poison of dissension between them that were honestly agreed, for before that time both the mind ruled the body without business, and the body obeyed without grudging. Now is it clean contrary. The order between them is so troubled, the affections or appetites of the body strive to go before reason, and reason is in a manner compelled to incline and follow the judgment of the body. mayst compare therefore a man properly to a commonalty, where is debate and part taking among themselves. Which commonalty for as much as it is made of sundry kinds of men gathered together, which be of diverse and contrary appetites: it cannot be avoided but that much strife shall arise therein, and parts taken often times, unless the chief rule and authority be in one. And he himself be such a fellow that will command nothing but that which shall be wholesome and profitable for the commonwealth. And for that cause it must needs be that he which is most wise should most bear rule. And he needs must obey that least perceiveth or understandeth. Now there is nothing more foolish than the rascal or vile commonalty. And therefore ought they to obey the officers and rulers, and bear no rule nor office themselves. The noble estates or such men which be most ancient of age, ought to be heard: but so that it lie only in the king's arbitrament to make statutes and laws, whom it is meet to be advertised to be put in remembrance or counselled now and then. But it is not meet that he should be compelled, or that any man should be master or rule him. finally the king obeyeth no man but the law only. The law must be correspondent to the original decree of nature or the first example of honesty. Wherefore if this order subverted, the unruly commons, and that raging dregs of the city shall strive to go before the seniors: or if the chief lords shall despise the commandment of the king, then ariseth perilous sedition or division in our commonwealth, yea and except the provision, decree or authority of God succour, all the matter weigheth and inclineth to extreme mischief and to utter destruction. man reason beareth the room of a king. Thou mayest account for the chief lords certain affections and them of the body: but yet not all things so beastly. the which kind is natural reverence toward the father and mother, love to thy brethren, a benevolent mind toward thy friends and lovers, compassion upon them that be vexed with adversity or cumbered with sickness, fear of infamy, slander or loss of thy good name, of honest reputation, and such other like. But such affections or passions which be very greatly disagreeing from the decrees of reason, and which be cast down and must bow even to the vileness of brute beasts: think and reckon those to be as it were the most rascal and vile sort of the common people. Of which kind and sort be lechery, riot, envy, and such like diseases, which all without exception must be kept under in prison and with punishment as vile and bond servants, that they render to their master their task and work appointed to them if they can: but if not at the least they do no harm. Which things Plato perceiving by inspiration of God, wrote in his book called Timeus how the sons of gods had forged in man to their own likeness two kinds of souls, the one kind spiritual and immortal, the other as it were mortal, in danger to divers perturbations or motions of unquietness. which the first is voluptuousness (as he saith) the bait whereby men are allured and brought to ungraciousness or mischief. The next is sorrow or grief which letteth men, and driveth them from virtue or goodness. After that fear and presumptuous boldness, two mad counsellors: whom accompanieth indurate wrath, the desire of vengeance. Moreover flattering hope with beastly imagination and knowledge not governed of reason, and worldly love that layeth hands violently on all things. These be almost the words of Plato, and it was not unknown to him the felicity of this life to be put in refraining of such perturbations, for he writeth in the same work them for to live justly and blessedly, which should have overcome these appetites, and them for to live unjustly and miserably that should be overcome of the same. to that soul which is like unto the nature of God, that is to say, unto reason, as unto a king, he appointed a place in the brain, as in the chief tower of our city: and as thou mayest see the highest part of our body, and next to heaven, and most far from the nature of a beast, as a thing verily which is both of a very thin bone, and neither laid with gross sinews nor flesh, but surely furnished and appointed within and also without, with powers of knowledge, that through the showing of them no debate should rise in our commonwealth, which he should not immediately perceive: but as touching the parts of the mortal soul, that is, to wit, the affections and appetites as every one of them is, either obedient, or else grudgeth against reason: he removed them from him, for between the neck and the midriff he set that part of the soul, wherein is contained boldness, wrath or anger, a seditious affection verily and full of debate, which needs must be refrained: but he is not very brutish or beastly, and therefore he separates him in a mean space from the highest and lowest, lest if he had been too nigh to either of them, he would either have troubled the king's quietness, or else corrupted with the contagiousness of them of the lowest sorts should with them also conspire against him. of all that power which desireth the voluptuous pleasure of meat and drink, whereby also we be moved to bodily lust, he banished utterly away far from the king's palace down alow beneath the midriff in to the liver and the paunch, that as it were a certain wild beast untamed he should there stable and dwell at the rack, for because that power is accustomed to raise up motions most violent, and to be disobedient to the commandments of the king. What beastliness yea and what rebellion is in the lowest portion of this power, at the leastway the privy parts of thy body may teach thee, in which part chiefly this power of concupiscence rageth and tyranny reigneth, which also of all members only ever among maketh rebellion with uncleanly motions, the king crying the contrary, and that in vain. Thou seest then evidently how that this noble beast man, so goodly a thing above plainly and without any exception endeth in an unreasonable or brute beast. that noble counsellor which sitteth like a king or a ruler in his high tower, having alway in remembrance his own beginning thinketh no filthy nor low thing. And he hath whereby he may be known from other a sceptre of ivory, because he doth command nothing but that which is right and good, in whose top writeth Homer to set an eagle, because that reason, mounting up to celestial things, beholdeth from above those things that be on the ground disdainfully, as it were with eagles' eyes. In conclusion he is crowned with a crown of gold, for gold in the mystical letters most commonly betokeneth wisdom. And the circle betokeneth that the wisdom of the king should be perfect and pure in every part. These be the very gifts or virtues properly belonging to kings. First that they be very wise that they do not amiss by reason of error and lack of true knowledge. And that such things as they know to be good and right, those only to will and purpose to do, that they do nothing against the decree or judgment of reason inordinately, frowardly and corruptly. And whosoever lacketh any of these two points, count him to be not a king, that is to say a ruler, but a robber.

Of the diversity of affections

CHAPTER V

OUR king Reason may be oppressed verily, yet because of the eternal law which God hath graven in him he cannot be corrupted but that he shall grudge and call back. whom, if the residue of the commonalty will obey, he shall never commit anything at all either to be repented or of any jeopardy: but all things shall be administered with great moderation discreetly, with much quietness and tranquillity. as touching affections, verily stoics and peripatetics vary somewhat, though both agree in this that we ought to live after reason, and not after affections. But stoics will when we have used for a season (as it were a schoolmaster to teach us our first principles) the affections which immediately are stirred up of the sensual powers, and now become to judgment and true examination what is to be ensured or chosen, what to be eschewed or forsaken, that then we utterly damn and forsake them. For then are they (as they say) not only no profit to very wisdom, but also hurtful and noxious, and therefore they will that a perfect wise man should lack all such motions, as diseases or sicknesses of the mind, yea and scarcely they grant to a wise man those first motions, more gentle preventing reason which they call fantasies or imaginations. Peripatetics teach the affections not to be destroyed utterly, but to be refrained, and that the use of them is not utterly to be refused, for because they think them to be given of nature, as a prick or a spur to stir a man to virtue: as wrath maketh a man bold and hardy, and is a matter of fortitude. Envy is a great cause of policy, and in likewise of the other. Socrates in a certain book that Plato made called Phedo seemeth to agree with stoics, where he thinketh philosophy to be nothing else but a meditation or practising of death, is to say that the mind withdraw herself as much as she can from corporal and sensible things, and convey herself to those things which be perceived with reason only, and not of the sensible powers. First of all therefore thou must behold and consider diligently all the motions, movings or stirring of thy mind and have them surely known. Furthermore thou must understand no motions to be so violent but they may be either refrained of reason, or else turned to virtue. Notwithstanding I hear everywhere this contagious opinion, that some should say they be constrained to vices: and on the other side many for lack of knowledge of themselves follow such motions as the sayings or decrees of reason: in so much that whatsoever wrath or envy doth counsel or move them to do, that they call the zeal of God: and as thou seest one commonwealth to be more unquiet than another: so is one man more inclined or prone to virtue than another, which difference cometh not of the diversity of minds, but either of the influence of celestial bodies, or else of our progenitors, or else of the bringing up in youth, or of the complexion of the body. The fable of Socrates of carters and horses good and bad is none old wives' tale: for thou mayst see some to be born of so moderate, soft, quiet and gentle disposition, so easy to be handled, to be turned and winded, that without business they may be induced to virtue, runneth forward by their own courage without any spurring. To some clean contrary thou mayst perceive to have happened: body rebellious as a wild and kicking horse: in so much that he which tameth him shall have enough to do and sweat apace, and yet scarce with a very rough bit, scarce with a waster and with sharp spurs can subdue his fierceness. If any such one hath happened to them, let never that, rather thy heart fail thee, but so much the more fervently set upon it, thinking on this wise: not that the way of virtue is stopped or shut up from thee: but a larger matter of virtue to be offered unto thee. But and if so be that nature hath endued thee with a gentle mind, thou art not therefore straightway better than another man, but happier, and yet again on that manner wise art thou more happy, so that thou art also more bound. How be it what is he that is endued with so happy gifts of nature, which hath not abundantly things enough to wrestle withal. Therefore in what part shall be perceived most rage or rebellion to be, in that part reason our king must watch diligently. be certain vices appropriate to every country, as to break promise is familiar to some: to some riot or prodigality: to some bodily lust or pleasure of the flesh, and this happeneth to them by the disposition of their countries. vices accompany the complexion of the body, as appetite and lust for the company of women and the desire of pleasures and wanton sports accompany the sanguine men. Wrath, fierceness, cursed speaking followeth the choleric men. Grossness of mind, lack of activity, sluggishness of body, and to be given to much sleep, followeth the phlegmatic man. Envy, inward heaviness, bitterness, to be solitary, self-minded, sullen and churlish followeth the melancholic person. vices abate and increase after the age of man, as in youth lust of the body, wasteful expenses and rashness, or foolish-hardiness. In old age niggardliness or too much saving, waywardness and avarice. vices there be which should seem appropriate to kind as fierceness to the man, vanity to the woman and desire of wreak, or to be revenged. It fortuneth now and then that nature, as it were to make amends, recompenseth one disease or sickness of the mind, another certian contrary good gift or property. One man is somewhat prone or inclined to pleasure of worldly pastimes, but nothing angry, nothing envious at all. Another is chaste, but somewhat proud or high-minded, somewhat hasty, somewhat too greedy upon the world. And there be which be vexed with certain wonderful and fatal vices, with theft, sacrilege and homicide: which truly thou must withstand with all thy might, against whose assault must be cast a certain brazen wall of sure purpose. On the other side some affections be so nigh neighbours to virtue, that it is jeopardous lest we should be deceived, the diversity is so dangerous and doubtful. affections are to be corrected and amended, and may be turned very well to that virtue which they most nigh resemble. There is some man (because of example) which is soon set a-fire, is hot, at once provoked to anger with the least thing in the world, let him refrain and sober his mind, and he shall be bold and courageous, nothing faint-hearted or fearful, he shall be free of speech without, dissimulation. There is another man somewhat holding, or too much saving, let him put to reason, and he shall be called thrifty and a good husband. He that is somewhat flattering shall be with moderation courtesy and pleasantness. He that is obstinate may be constant. Solemness may be turned to gravity. And that hath too much of foolish toys, may be a good companion. after the same manner of other somewhat easier diseases of the mind, we must beware of this only that we cloak not the vice of nature with the name of virtue, calling heaviness of mind gravity, cruelty justice, envy zeal, filthy niggardliness thrift, flattering good fellowship, knavery or ribaldry urbanity or merry speaking. The only way therefore to felicity is first that thou know thyself: that thou do nothing after affections, but in all things after the judgment of reason: reason be sound and pure and without corruption: let not his mouth be out of taste, that is to say, let him behold honest things. But thou wilt say: it is an hard thing that thou commandest: who sayeth nay? And verily the saying of Plato is true: whatsoever things be fair and honest, the same be hard and travailful to obtain. Nothing is more hard than that a man should overcome himself. But then is there no greater reward than is felicity? s spake that thing excellently as he doth all other things: nothing is more happy than a christian man, to whom is promised the kingdom of heaven: nothing is in greater peril than he which every hour is in jeopardy of his life: nothing is more strong than he that overcometh the devil: nothing is more weak than he that is overcome of the flesh. If thou ponder thine own strength only, nothing is harder than to subdue the flesh unto the spirit. If thou shalt look on God thy helper, nothing is more easy. Then now therefore conceive with all thy might and with a fervent mind the purpose and profession of the perfect life. And when thou hast grounded thyself upon a sure purpose, set upon it and go to it lustily: man's mind never purposed anything fervently that he was not able to bring to pass. is a great part of a christian life to desire with full purpose and with all his heart to be a christian man, that thing which at the first sight or meeting, at the first acquaintance or coming to shall seem impossible to be conquered or won, in process of time shall be gentle enough and with use easy: in conclusion with custom it shall be very pleasant. It is a very proper saying of Hesiodus: way of virtue is hard at the beginning, but after thou hast crept up to the top there remaineth for thee very sure quietness. No beast is so wild which waxeth not tame by the craft of man. And is there no craft to tame the mind of him that is the tamer of all things? That thou might be whole in thy body, thou canst steadfastly purpose and command thyself for certain years to abstain from drinking of wine, to forbear the flesh and company of women: which things the physician being a man prescribed to thee. And to live quietly all thy life canst thou not rule thine affections, no not a few months? Which thing God, that is thy creator and maker, commandeth thee to do? To save thy body from sickness there is nothing which thou doeth not: to deliver thy body and thy soul also from eternal death dost thou not these things which infidels, ethnics and gentiles have done.

Of the inward and outward man and of the
two parts of man, proved by holy scripture

CHAPTER VI

CERTAINLY I am ashamed in christian men's behalf, of whom the most part follow as they were brute beasts, their affections and sensual appetites, and in this kind of war are so rude and unexercised, that they do not as much as know the diversity between reason and affections or passions. They suppose the thing only to be the man which they see and feel and they think nothing to be beside the things which offer themselves to the sensible wits when it is nothing less than so. What so ever they greatly covet, that they think to be right: they call peace, certain and assured bondage, while reason oppressed and blinded followeth whither so ever the appetite or affection calleth, without resistance. This is that miserable peace which Christ, the author of very peace that knit two in one, came to break, stirring up a wholesome war between the father and the son, between the husband and the wife, between those things which filthy concord had evil-coupled together. Now then let the authority of the philosophers be of little weight, except those same things be all taught in holy scripture, though not with the same words. the philosophers call reason, that calleth Paul, sometime the spirit, sometime the inner man, other while the law of the mind. That they call affection, he calleth sometime the flesh: sometime the body: another time the outer man, and the law of the members. Walk (saith Paul) in the spirit, and ye shall not accomplish the desires and lusts of the flesh, for the flesh desireth contrary to the spirit, and the spirit contrary to the flesh, that ye cannot do whatsoever things ye would. And in another place: ye shall live after the flesh, ye shall die. If ye shall, walking in the spirit, mortify the deeds of the flesh, ye shall live. Certainly this is a new change of things, that peace should be sought in war, and war in peace: in death life, and in life death: in bondage liberty, in liberty bondage. Paul writeth in another place: I chastise my body and bring him into servitude. Hear also the liberty. If ye be led with the spirit, ye be not subject to the law. And we have not (saith he) received again the spirit of bondage in fear, but the spirit which hath elected us to be the children of God. He saith in another place: I see another law in my members repugnynge against the law of my mind, subduing me to the law of sin which law is in my members. Thou readest with him also of the outer man which is corrupt, and of the inner man which is renewed day by day. Plato put two souls to be in one man. Paul in one man maketh two men so coupled together, that neither without other can be either in heaven or hell: again so separate that the death of the one should be life of the other. To the same (as I suppose) pertain those things which he wrote to the Chorintes. The first man was made into a living soul. last Adam was made into a spirit quickening: but that is not first which is spiritual, but that which is living: then followeth that which is spiritual. The first man came of the earth himself terrestrial. The second came from heaven and he himself celestial. And because it should more evidently appear these things to pertain not only to Christ and Adam, but to us all, he added saying: As was the man of the earth, such are terrestrial and earthly persons. As is the celestial man, such are the celestial persons. Therefore as we have borne the image of the earthly man: even so now let us bear the image of the celestial man. For this I say, brethren, that flesh and blood shall not possess the kingdom of heaven, nor corruption shall possess incorruption. perceivest plainly how in this place he calleth Adam made of earth that thing which in another place he calleth the flesh and the outer man which is corrupt. And this same thing certainly is also the body of death, wherewith Paul aggrieved cried out: Oh wretch that I am, who shall deliver me from this body of death? In conclusion Paul declaring the most diverse fruit of the flesh and of the spirit writeth in another place, saying: He that followeth in his flesh shall reap or mow of his flesh corruption: but he that soweth in the spirit shall reap or mow of the spirit life eternal. This is the old debate of two twins Jacob and Esau, which before they were brought forth into light wrestled within the cloisters of the mother's belly, and Esau verily caught from Jacob the preeminence of birth and was first-born: but Jacob prevented him again of his father's blessing. That which is carnal cometh first, but the spiritual thing is ever best. The one was red, high coloured and rough with hair: the other smooth. The one unquiet and a hunter: the other rejoiced in domestical quietness. And the one also for hunger sold the right that pertained to him by inheritance, in that he was the elder brother, while he, enticed with a vile price and reward of voluptuousness, fell from his native liberty into the bondage of sin. The other procured by craft of grace that which belonged not to him by right of law. Between these two brethren though both were born of one belly, and at one time, yet was there never joined perfect concord. For Esau hateth Jacob, Jacob for his part, though he quitteth not hate for hate, yet he fleeth and hath ever Esau suspected, neither dare come within his danger. To thee likewise what so ever thing affection counselleth or persuadeth: let it be suspected, for the doubtful credence of the counsellor. Jacob only saw the Lord: Esau as one delighting in blood liveth by the sword. To conclude, when the mother asked counsel of the Lord he answered: the elder shall be servant to the younger: the father Isaac added: thou Esau shalt do service to thy brother: and the time shall come when thou shalt shake off and loose his yoke from thy neck. The Lord prophesieth of good and obedient persons, the father of evil and disobedient persons. The one declareth what ought to be done of all men: the other told aforehand what the most part would do. Paul willeth that the wife be obedient to her husband: for better is (saith scripture) the iniquity of the man than the goodness of the woman. Eve is carnal affection, whose eyes the subtle and crafty serpent daily troubleth and vexeth with temptation, and she once corrupted goeth forth and ceaseth not to provoke and entice the man also through consent to be partaker of the iniquity or mischievous deed. But what readest thou of the new woman, of her I mean that is obedient to her husband? I will put hatred between thee (meaning the serpent and the woman) and between her generation and thine, shall tread down thy head and thou shalt lay await to her heel. serpent was cast down on his breast, the death of Christ weakened his violence, he now only lieth await to her heel privily. But the woman through grace of faith changed as it were into a man boldly treadeth down his venomous head. Grace is increased and the tyranny of the flesh is diminished. When Sara was minished and decayed, then did Abraham (God being the author) grow and increase. And then she calleth him not husband but lord, neither yet could she obtain to have a child before she was dried up and barren. What I pray thee brought she forth at the last to her lord Abraham now in her old days, yea, and past child bearing? Verily Isaac, that is to say joy, for as soon as affections have waxed old and are weakened in a man, then at the last springeth up the blessed tranquillity of an innocent mind, with sure quietness of the spirit, as it were a continual feast. And as the father let not his wife have her pleasure without advisement: even so hath the sporting of the children together suspect, I mean of Isaac with Ismael. Sara would not the child of a bondwoman and the child of a free woman should have conversation together at that age: but that Ismael (while as yet youth is fervent) should be banished out of presence, lest under a colour of pastime he might entice and draw into his own manners Isaac yet young and tender of age. was Sara an old wife and now had brought forth Isaac, yet mistrusteth Abraham except the answer of God had approved his wife's counsel, he is not sure of the woman until he heard of God: In all things that Sara hath said to thee, hear her voice. O happy old age of them in whom so mortified is the carnal man made of the earth, that he in nothing defieth the spirit, which agreement whether in all things perfect may happen to any man in this life or no, verily I dare not affirm, ure it were not expedient, for even unto Paul was given unquietness and trouble of the flesh, the messenger of Satan, to vex him withal. And at the third time he refused to have the messenger taken from him. Then had he none other answer of God but only this: Paul, my grace is sufficient for thee. For strength is wrought and made perfect in weakness. Indeed this is a new kind of remedy. Paul, lest he should be proud, is tempted with pride, that he might be strong in Christ: he is compelled to be weak in himself: he bare the treasure of celestial revelations in a vessel of earth, that the excellency should depend on the might of God, and not on himself, which one example of the apostle putteth us in remembrance and warneth us of many things. of all that when we be assaulted of vices, immediately we must give ourselves to prayer again, and desire help of God. that temptations to perfect men are not perilous: but also are very expedient to the continuance and preserving of virtue. Last of all when all other things are full tamed then the vice of vainglory even in the chief time of virtues layeth await: and this vice to be as it were Hydra, whom Hercules fought withal, a quick monster long of life and fruitful, by reason of her own wounds, which at the last end, when all labours be overcome, can scarce be destroyed. Nevertheless continual and importunate labour overcometh all thing. In the meantime while thy mind rageth and is vexed with vehement perturbations, by all manner of means thrust together, draw down, hold and bind this Protheus with tough bands while he goeth about to change himself into all manner monsters and affections of things, fire, into the shape of some terrible wild beast and into a running river, until he come again into his own natural likeness and shape. What is so like Protheus as is the affections and appetites of fools, which draw them sometime into beastly and bodily lust, sometime into mad ire or wrath, otherwhiles into poison, envy and strange fashions of vices? Agreeth it not well that the excellent cunning poet Virgil said: There shall diveirse similitudes and fashions of wild beasts delude and mock, for suddenly he will be a fearful swine and foul tiger, and a dragon full of scales, and a lioness with a red mane, or shall counterfeit the quick sound of the flame of fire. But here have in remembrance what followeth. The more he changeth himself into all manner of similitudes, the more, my son (saith Virgil), strain thy tough bands. And also because we shall not need to return again to fables of poets, thou shalt by the example of the holy patriarch

Jacob learn to endure and to wrestle lustily all night until the morning, by the help of God, begin to give light. And thou shalt say, I will not let thee depart except thou shalt have given me thy blessing first. But what reward of his victory and great virtue that mighty and excellent strong wrestler obtained, it is certainly very profitable to hear. First of all God blessed him in that same place. evermore after that the temptation is overcome, a certain singular increase of divine grace is added unto a man, whereby he should be another time much more surely armed than he was before against the assault of his enemy. Furthermore through touching of the thigh the sinew of the conqueror waxed withered and shrunk, and he began to halt on the one foot. God curseth them by the mouth of his prophet which halt on both their feet, that is to say, them which will both live carnally, and please God also. But they be happy in whom carnal affections be so mortified, that they bear and lean most of all to the right foot, that is, to the spirit. Finally, his name was changed: of Jacob he was made Israel, and of a busy wrestler a quiet person. that thou hast chastised thy flesh or thy body, and crucified him with vices and concupiscences, then shall tranquillity and quietness without all trouble come unto thee, that thou mayst be at leisure to behold the Lord, that thou mayst taste and feel that the Lord is pleasant and sweet, for that thing is signified by Israel. God is not seen in fire, neither in the whirlwind and troublous rage of temptation, but after the tempest of the devil (if so be that thou shalt endure perseveringly) followeth the hissing of a thin air or wind of spiritual consolation. After that air hath breathed quietly upon thee, then apply thine inward eyes, and thou shalt be Israel, and shalt say with him, I have seen my Lord, and my soul is made whole. Thou shalt see him that said: No flesh shall see me, that is to say, no carnal man. Consider thyself diligently, if thou be flesh, thou shalt not see God: if thou see him not, thy soul shall not be made whole. Take heed therefore that thou be a spirit.

Of three parts of man, the spirit, the soul, and the flesh

CHAPTER VII

THESE things afore written had been and that a great deal more than sufficient: ess that thou mayst be somewhat more sensibly known unto thyself, I
will rehearse compendiously the division of a man, after the description of
Origene, for he followeth Paul making three parts, the spirit, the soul and the
flesh, which three parts Paul joined together, writing to the Thessalonieences.
That your spirit (saith he) your soul and your body may be kept clean and
uncorrupt, that ye be not blamed or accused at the coming of our Lord Jesu
Christ. And Esaias (leaving out the lowest part) maketh mention of two,
saying, My soul shall desire and long for thee in the night, yea, and in my
spirit and my heart strings I will wake in the mornings for to please thee. Also
Daniel saith, Let the spirits and souls of good men laud God. of the which
places of scripture Origene gathereth not against reason the three partitions of
man, that is to wit, the body, otherwise called the flesh, the most vile part of
us, wherein the malicious serpent through original trespass hath I written the
law of sin, wherewithal we be provoked to filthiness. And also if we be overcome, we be coupled and made one with the devil. the spirit wherein we
represent the similitude of the nature of God, in which also our most blessed
maker after the original pattern and example of his own mind hath graven the
eternal law of honesty with his finger, that is, with his spirit the Holy Ghost.
By this part we be knit to God, and made one with him. In the third place,
and in the midst between these two he putteth the soul, which is partaker of
the sensible wits and natural motions. is in a seditious and wrangling 'commonwealth and must needs join herself to the one part or the other, she is
troubled of both parts, she is at her liberty to whether part she will incline. If
she forsake the flesh and convey herself to the parts of the spirit, she herself
shall be spiritual also. But if she cast herself down to the appetites of the body
she shall grow out of kind into the manner of the body. This is it that Paul

meant writing to the Chorintes. Remember ye not that he that joineth himself to an harlot is made one body with her: but he that cleaveth to the Lord, is one spirit with him. He calleth the harlot the frail and weak part of the man. is that pleasant and flattering woman of whom thou readest in the second chapter of Proverbs on this wise. That thou mayst be delivered from a strange woman and from a woman of another country, which maketh her words sweet and pleasant, and forsaketh her husband to whom she was married in her youth, and hath forgot the promise she made to her Lord God: her house boweth down to death and her path is to hell. Whosoever goeth into hell, shall never return: nor shall attain the path of life. And in the vi. chapter. That thou mayst keep thee from an evil woman, and from the flattering tongue of a strange woman, let not thy heart melt on her beauty, be not thou deceived with her beckonings, for the price of an harlot is scarce worth a piece of bread: but the woman taketh away the precious soul of the man. Did he not when he made mention of the harlot, the heart and the soul express by name three parts of the man? Again, in the ix. chapter: A foolish woman ever babbling and full of words, swimming in pleasures, and hath no learning at all, sitteth in the doors of her house upon a stool in a high place of the city to call them that pass by the way and be going in their journey, Whosoever is a child, let him turn in to me: and she said unto a fool and an heartless person, Water that is stolen is pleasanter, and bread that is hid privily is sweeter. And he was not aware that there be giants, and their jests be in the bottom of hell. For whosoever shall be coupled to her, he shall descend into hell. And whosoever shall depart from her, shall be saved. I beseech thee with what colours could more workmanly have been painted and set out either the venomous enticements and wanton pleasures of the poisoned flesh, provoking and tempting the soul to filthiness of sin, or else the importunity of the same crying and striving against the spirit, or the wretched end that followeth when she doth overcome the spirit. To conclude therefore, the spirit maketh us gods, the flesh maketh us beasts: the soul maketh us men: the spirit maketh us religious, obedient to God, kind and merciful. The flesh maketh us despisers of God, disobedient to God, unkind and cruel. The soul maketh us indifferent, that is to say, neither good nor bad. The spirit desireth celestial things: the flesh desireth delicate and pleasant things: the soul desireth necessary things: the spirit carryeth us up to heaven: the flesh thrusteth us down to hell. To the soul nothing is imputed, that is to say, it doth neither good nor harm: whatsoever is carnal or springeth of the flesh that is filthy: whatsoever is spiritual proceeding of the spirit, that is pure, perfect and godly: whatsoever is natural and proceedeth of the soul, is a medium and indifferent thing, neither good nor bad. Wilt thou more plainly have the diversity of these three parts shewed unto thee as it were with a man's finger? Certainly I will essay. doest reverence to thy father and mother: thou lovest thy brother, thy children and thy friend: it is not of so great virtue to do these things, as it is abominable not to do them. For why shouldest thou not being a christian man do that thing which the gentiles by the teaching of nature do, yea which brute beasts do? That thing that is natural shall not be imputed unto merit. But thou art come in to such a strait case that either the reverence toward thy father must be despised, the inward love towards thy children must be subdued, the benevolence to thy friend set at nought, or God must be offended. What wilt thou now do? The soul standeth in the midst between two ways: the flesh crieth upon her on the one side, the spirit on the other side. The spirit saith, God is above thy father: thou art bound to thy father but for thy body only. To God thou art bound for all thing that thou hast. The flesh putteth thee in remembrance, saying: Except thou obey thy father, he will disinherit thee, thou shalt be called of every man an unkind and unnatural child, look to thy profit, have respect to thy good name and fame. God either doth not see, or else dissimuleth and wittingly looketh beside it, or at the least, will be soon pacified again. thy soul doubteth, now she wavereth hither and thither, to whether of either part she turn herself. That same shall she be, that that thing is she went unto. If she obey the harlot, that is to say the flesh (the spirit despised) she shall be one body with the flesh. But if she lift up herself and ascend to the spirit (the flesh set at nought) she shall be transposed and changed to the nature of the spirit. After this manner accustom to examine thyself prudently. The error of those men is exceeding great which oftentimes weeneth that thing to be perfect virtue and goodness which is but of nature and no virtue at all. affections somewhat honest in appearance, and as they were disguised with visors of virtue, deceiveth negligent persons. The judge is hasty and cruel against the felon, or him that hath trespassed the law, he seemeth to himself constant and of gravity uncorrupt and a man of good conscience, wilt thou have this man discussed? If he favour his own mind too much and follow a certain natural rigorousness without any grief of mind, perad venture with some pleasure or delectation: yet not leaning from the office and duty of a judge, let him not forthwith stand too much in his own conceit: it is an indifferent thing that he doth. But if he abuse the law for private hate or lucre, now it is carnal that he doth, and he committeth murder. But and if he feel great sorrow in his mind because he is compelled to destroy and kill him, whom he had liefer amended and saved: also if he enjoin punishment according to the trespass with such a mind, with such sorrow of heart, as the father commandeth his singularly beloved son to be cut, lanced or seared: of this manner shall it be spiritual that he doth. most part of men through proneness of nature and some special property, either rejoice in, or abhor certain things. Some there be whom bodily lust tickleth not at all: let not them by and by ascribe that unto virtue which is an indifferent thing, for not to lack bodily lust, but to overcome bodily lust is the office of virtue. man hath a pleasure to fast, a pleasure to be at mass, a pleasure to be much at church and to say a great deal of psalmody: examine after this rule that thing which he doeth: if he regard the common fame or advantage, it smelleth of the flesh and not of the spirit: if he do follow but his own inclination (for he doth that which pleaseth his own mind) then he hath not whereof he so ought greatly to rejoice, rather whereof he ought to fear. Behold a jeopardous thing unto thyself. Thou prayest, and judgest him that prayeth not. Thou fasteth, and condemneth him that fasteth not. Whosoever doeth not that thou doest, thou thinkest thyself better than he: beware lest thy fast pertain to thy flesh. Thy brother hath need of thy help, thou in the mean space mumblest in thy prayers unto God, and wilt not be known of thy brother's necessity. God shall abhor these prayers: for how shall God hear thee while thou prayest, when thou which art a man canst not find in thy heart to hear another man. Perceive also another thing. Thou lovest thy wife for this cause only, that she is thy wife. Thou doest no great thing, for this thing is common as well to infidels as to thee: or else thou lovest her for none other thing but because she is to thee pleasant and delectable. Thy love now draweth to thee fleshward. thou lovest her for this thing chiefly, because thou hast perceived in her the image of Christ, which is godly reverence, modesty, soberness, chastity: and now lovest not her in her self but in Christ: yea rather Christ in her. After this manner lovest spiritually. Notwithstanding we shall say more of these things in their places.

Certain general rules of true christian living

CHAPTER VIII

NOW for because we have opened as me seemeth the way (howsoever we have done it), and have prepared as it were certain stuff and matter unto the thing which was purposed, we must haste to that which remaineth, lest it should not be an Enchiridion, is to say, a little treatise handsome to be carried in a man's hand, but rather a great volume; we will enforce to give certain rules, as they were certain points of wrestling, by whose guiding and conveyance, as it were by the guiding of the thread of Dedalus, men may easily plunge up out of the blind errors of this world, as out of Labirinthus, which is a certain cumbrous maze, and come into the pure and clear light of spiritual living. None other science is there which hath not her rules. And shall the craft of blessed living only be without the help of all manner of precepts? is without fail a certain craft of virtuous living and a discipline, in which whosoever exercise themselves manfully, them shall favour that Holy Spirit, which is the promoter and bringer forward of all holy enforcement and godly purposes. But whosoever saith, Depart from us we will not have the knowledge of thy ways: these men the mercy of God refuseth, because they first have refused knowledge. These rules shall be taken partly of the person of God, of the person of the devil, and of our person, partly of things, that is to say, of virtues and vices, and of things to them annexed, partly of the matter or stuff whereof virtues or vices be wrought. They shall profit singularly against the evil things remaining of original sin. For though baptism hath wiped away the spot, yet there cleaveth still in us a certain thing of the old disease left behind, both partly for the custody of humility, and also for the matter and increase of virtue. These be blindness, the flesh and infirmity or weakness. Blindness with the mist of ignorance dimmeth the judgment of reason. For partly the sin of our first progenitors hath not a little dusked that so pure a light of the countenance, resemblance, or similitude of God, which our creator hath shewed upon us.

much more corrupt bringing up, lewd company, froward affections, darkness of vices, custom of sin hath so cankered it, that of the law graven in us of God scarce any signs or tokens doth appear. Then as I began, blindness causeth that we in the election of things be as good as half blinded and deceived with error, in the stead of the best, following the worst, preferring things of less value before things of greater price. The flesh troubleth the affection so much, that even though we know what is best, yet love we the contrary. Infirmity and weakness maketh us that we being overcome either with tediousness or with temptation, forsake the virtue which we had once gotten and attained. Blindness hurteth the judgment, the flesh corrupteth the will, infirmity weakeneth constancy. first point therefore is that thou can discern things to be refused from things to be accepted: and therefore blindness must be taken away lest we stumble or stagger in the election of things. The next is, that thou hate the evil as soon as it is once known, and love that which is honest and good: and in this thing the flesh must he overcome, lest contrary to the judgment of the mind we should love sweet and delectable things in the stead of wholesome things. third is, that we continue in these things which we began well: and therefore the weakness must be underset, lest we forsake the way of virtue with greater shame than if we had been never about to walk or enter therein. Ignorance must be remedied, that thou mayst see which way to go. The flesh must be tamed, lest she lead thee aside out of the highway, once known, into bypaths. Weakness must be comforted, lest when thou hast entered into the strait way thou shouldst either faint or stop or turn back again, or lest after thou hast once set thy hand to the plough shouldst look backward, but shouldst rejoice as a strong giant to haste the way, ever stretching forth thyself to those things which be afore thee, without remembrance of those things which be behind thee, until thou mayst lay hand on the reward appointed and on the crown promised to them that continue unto these three things: therefore we shall apply certain rules according to our little power.

Against the evil of ignorance. The first rule

CHAPTER IX

BUT inasmuch as faith is the only gate unto Christ, the first rule must be that thou judge very well both of him and also of scripture given by his spirit, and that thou believe not with mouth only, not faintly, not negligently, not doubtfully, as the common rascal of christian men do: but let it be set fast and immovable throughout all thy breast, not one jot to be contained in them that appertaineth not greatly unto thy health. it move thee nothing at all that thou seest a great part of men so live, as though heaven and hell were but some manner of tales of old wives, to fear or flatter young children withal: but believe thou surely and make no haste, the whole world should be mad at once, though the elements should be changed, though the angels should rebel: yet verity cannot lie, it cannot but come which God told before should come. If thou believe he is God, thou must needs believe that he is true also, and on this wise think without wavering, nothing to be so true, nothing to be so sure, and without doubt of the things which thou nearest with thine ears, which thou presently beholdest with thine eyes, which thou handlest with thy hands, as those things be true which thou readest in the scriptures, that God of heaven, that is to say verity, gave by inspiration, which the holy prophets brought forth, and the blood of so many martyrs hath approved: unto which now so many hundred years the consent of all good men hath agreed and set their seals: which Christ here being in flesh, both taught in his doctrine and expressly represented or counterfeited in his manners and living. Unto which also miracles bear witness, the devils confess and so much believe, that they quake and tremble for fear. Last of all which be so agreeable unto the equity of nature, which so agree between themselves, and be everywhere like themselves, which so ravisheth the minds of them that attend, so moveth and changeth them. If these so great tokens agree unto them alone, what devil's madness is it to doubt in the faith? Yea of those things past thou mayst easily conjecture what shall follow: how many and great things also, how incredible to be spoken did the prophets tell before of Christ: which of these things came not to pass? Shall he in other things deceive which in them deceived not? In conclusion, the prophets lied not, and shall Christ the Lord of prophets lie? If with this and such other like cogitations thou often stir up the flame of faith, and then fervently desire of God to increase thy faith, I shall marvel if thou canst be any long time an evil man. For who is all together so unhappy and full of mischief that would not depart from vices, if so be he utterly believed, that with these momentary pleasures, beside the unhappy vexation of conscience and mind, is purchased also eternal punishments: on the other side, if he surely believed for this temporal and little worldly vexation to be rewarded or recompensed to good men an hundred fold joy of pure conscience presently: and at the last life immortal.

The second rule

CHAPTER X

LET the first point be therefore that thou doubt in no wise of the promises of God. next that thou go unto the way of life, not slothfully, not fearfully: but with sure purpose, with all thy heart, with a confident mind, and (if I may so say) with such mind as he hath that would rather fight than drink: so that thou be ready at all hours for Christ's sake to lose both life and goods. A slothful man will and will not. The kingdom of heaven is not gotten of negligent and reckless persons, but plainly rejoiceth to suffer violence: and violent persons violently obtain it. Suffer not the affection of them whom thou lovest singularly to hold thee back hasting thither ward: let not the pleasures of this world call thee back again: not the care of thy household be any hindrance to thee. The chain of worldly business must be cut asunder, for surely it cannot otherwise be loosed. must be forsaken in such a manner that thou turn not again in thy mind at any time unto the pots of the flesh. Sodoma must be forsaken utterly hastily, yea, and at once: it is not lawful to look back. The woman looked back and she was turned into the image of a stone. The man had no leisure anywhere to abide in any region, but was commanded to haste into the mountain, unless that he had liefer to have perished. The prophet crieth out that we should flee out of the midst of Babylon. departing of the Israelytes from Egypt is called flight or running away. We be commanded to flee out of Babylon hastily, and not to remove a little and a little slowly. Thou mayst see the most part of men prolong the time, and with very slow purpose go about to flee from vices. When I have once rid myself out of such and such matters, say they, yea when I have brought that and that business to pass. Oh fool, what and if God this same day take again thy soul from thee? Perceivest thou not one business to rise of another, and one vice to call in another? Why rather doest thou not today that thing which the sooner thou doest, the easier shall it be done? Be diligent some other where. In this matter to do rashly, to run headlong and suddenly, is chiefest of all and most profitable. not nor ponder how much thou forsakest, but be sure Christ only shall be sufficient for all things: only be bold to commit thyself to him with all thine heart: thou mistrust in thine own self, adventure to put unto him all the governance of thyself: trust to thyself no longer, but with full confidence cast thyself from thyself to him, and he shall receive thee: commit thy care and thought to the Lord, he shall nourish thee up, that thou mayst sing the song of the same prophet. The Lord is my governor, and I shall lack nothing. In a place of pasture he hath set me, by the water side of comfort he hath brought up me: he hath converted my soul. Be not minded to part thyself into two, to the world and to Christ: thou canst not serve two masters: there is no fellowship between God and Belial. God cannot away with them which halt on both their legs: his stomach abhorreth them which be neither hot nor cold, but lukewarm. God is a very jealous lover of souls: he will possess only and altogether that thing which he redeemed with his blood: he cannot suffer the fellowship of the devil, whom he once overcame with death. be but two ways only, the one which by obedience of the affections leadeth to perdition: the other which through mortifying of the flesh, leadeth to life. Why doubtest thou in thyself, there is no third way, into one of these two thou must needs enter, wilt thou or wilt thou not, whatsoever thou art, or of what degree, thou must needs enter into this strait way, in which few mortal men walk? But this way Christ himself hath trod, and have trodden since the world began whosoever pleased God. is doubtless the inevitable necessity of the goddess Adrastia, otherwise called Nemesis or Rhamnusia, that is to say, it cannot be chosen but that thou be crucified with Christ as touching the world, if thou purpose to live with Christ. Why like fools flatter we ourselves, why in so weighty a matter deceive we ourselves? One saith, I am not of the clergy or a spiritual man, I am of the world, I cannot but use the world. Another thinketh, though I be a priest yet am I no monk, let him look upon it. And the monk also hath found a thing to flatter himself withal, though I be a monk yet am I not of so strait an order as such and such. Another saith, I am a young man, I am a gentleman, I am rich, I am a courtier, and to be short, a prince, those things pertain not to me which were spoken to the apostles. wretch, then appertaineth it nothing to thee that thou shouldst live in Christ? If thou be in the world, in Christ thou art not: if thou call the sky, the earth, the sea and this common air the world: so is there no man which is not in the world: and if thou call the world ambition, that is to say, desire of honour, promotion, or authority: if thou call the world pleasures, covetousness, bodily lust: certainly if thou be worldly, thou art not a christian man. Christ spake indifferently to all men: whosoever would not take his cross

and follow him, could be no meet man for him, or be his disciple: die with
Christ as touching the flesh is nothing to thee, if to live by his spirit pertaineth
nothing to thee: to be crucified as touching the world pertaineth nothing to
thee, if to live godly or in God, pertain nothing to thee: to be buried together
with Christ belongeth nothing to thee, if to arise again to eternal glory belong
nothing to thee: the humility, poverty, tribulation, vile reputation, the laborious agonies and sorrows of Christ, pertain nothing at all unto thee, if the
kingdom of him pertain nothing unto thee. What can be more lewd than to
think the reward to be common as well to thee as to other: and yet nevertheless
to put the labours whereby the reward is obtained, from thee, to a certain few
persons? What can be more a wanton thing than to desire to reign with the
Head, and yet wilt thou take no pain with him? Therefore, my brother, look
not so greatly what other men do, and in comparison of them flatter or please
thyself. To die as touching sin: to die as touching carnal desires: to die as
touching the world is a certain hard thing and known to very few, yea though
they be monks, yet this is the common or general profession of all christian
men. This thing a great while agone thou hast sworn and holily promised in
the time of baptism: than which vow what other thing can there be either
more holy or religious? Either we must perish, or else without exception we
must go this way to health, whether we be knights or ploughmen. Notwithstanding though it fortune not to all men to attain the perfect counterfeiting or
following of the Head, yet all must enforce with feet and hands to come thereto. He hath a great part of a christian man's living, which with all his heart,
with a sure and steadfast purpose, hath determined to be a christian man.

The third rule

CHAPTER XI

BUT lest that thing fear thee from the way of virtue because it seemeth sharp
and grievous, partly because thou must forsake worldly commodities, partly
because thou must fight continually against three very cruel enemies, the flesh,
the devil, and the world, set this third rule before thee alway, bear thyself in
hand that all the fearful things and fantasies which appear forthwith unto thee
as it were in the first entering of hell ought to be counted for a thing of
nought, the example of Virgilius' Eneas. For certainly, if thou shalt consider
the very thing somewhat groundly and steadfastly (setting at nought these
apparent things which beguiled thine eyes) thou shalt perceive that none other
way is more commodious than the way of Christ: though thou account this
thing not at all, that this way only leadeth to eternal life, yea and though thou
have no respect unto the reward. For I beseech thee what kind of living after
the common course of the world is there that thou canst choose in which thou
shall not bear and suffer things enough abundantly both careful and grievous?
Who is he that knoweth not the life of courtiers to be full of grievous labour
and wretched misery, except it be either he that never proved it or certainly a
very natural fool? Oh immortal God, what bondage, how long and how ungoodly must there be suffered even unto the life's end! What a cumbrous
business is there in seeking in purchasing the prince's love and grace! A man
must flatter to obtain the favour of all such as may either hinder or further
one. The countenances must now and then be feigned and new fashioned.
injuries of the greater men must be whispered or muttered with silence secretly. Consequently, what kind of evil life can be imagined whereof the life of
warriors is not full? Of either life then mayst thou be a very good witness,
which hast learned both at thine own peril. as touching the merchant man
what is that he either doth not or suffereth not fleeing poverty by sea, by land,
through fire and water? matrimony what a mountain of household cares be

there? misery feel not they there which proveth and hath experience of it! In bearing of offices how much vexation, how much labour, and how much peril is there! which way so ever thou turn thyself an huge company of incommodities meeteth thee. The very life of mortal men of itself without addition of any other thing is cumbered and tangled with a thousand miseries which be common and indifferent as well to good as bad. all shall grow into a great heap of merits unto thee if they shall find thee in the way of Christ: if not they shall be the more grievous, moreover fruitless, and yet must nevertheless be suffered. Whosoever be soldiers of this world, first how many years do they pant, blow, sweat, and canvass the world, tormenting themselves with thought and care, moreover for how transitory and things of naught? Last of all, in how doubtful hope? Add to this that there is no rest or easement of miseries, in so much that the more they have laboured, the more grievous is the pain. And when all is past, what shall the end be of so tedious and laborious a life? verily eternal punishment. So now and with this life compare the way of virtue, which at the first ceaseth to be tedious, in process is made easier, is made pleasant and delectable, by which way also we go with very sure hope to eternal felicity. Were it not the uttermost madness to have liefer with equal labour to purchase eternal death rather than life immortal? are these worldly men much madder than so, that they choose with extreme labour to go to labour everlasting, rather than with less labours to go to immortal quietness. Moreover if the way of piety, or obedience to God were so much more laborious than the way of the world, yet here the grievousness of the labour is assuaged with hope of reward, and the comfort of God is not lacking which turneth the bitterness of the gall into the sweetness of honey. There one care calleth in another, of one sorrow springeth another, no quietness is there at all. The labour and affliction withoutforth, the grievous cares and thoughts withinforth cause the very easements to be sharp and bitter. These things so to be was not unknown to the poets of the gentiles which, by the punishment of Ticius, Ixion, Tantalus, Sisiphus, and of Pentheus, painted and described the miserable and grievous life of lewd and wretched persons: of whom is also the late confession in the book of Sapyence. We be wearied in the way of iniquity and perdition, we have walked hard ways, but the way of God we know not. What could be either filthier or more laborious than the servitude of Egypt? What could be more grievous than the captivity of Babylon? What more intolerable than the yoke of Pharao and of Nabugodonosor? But what saith Christ? Take my yoke upon your necks and ye shall find rest unto your souls: my yoke, saith he, is pleasant and my burden light. To speak briefly, no pleasure is lacking where is not lacking a quiet conscience. No misery is there lacking where an unhappy conscience crucifieth the mind. These things must be taken as of most certainty, but and if thou yet doubt go ask of them which in time past have been converted out of the middle of Babylon, unto the Lord: and by experience of them at the least way believe nothing to be more troublous and grievous than vices, nothing to be more easy or of quicker speed than not to be drowned in business, nothing more cheerful and more comfortable than is virtue. Nevertheless go to let it be that the wages be like, and that the labours be like also, yet for all that how greatly ought a man to desire to war under the standard of Christ, rather than under the banners of the devil. Yea, how much liefer were it to be vexed or to suffer affliction with Christ, than to swim in pleasures with the devil. Moreover, ought not a man with wind and weather, with ship sail and swiftness of horses, to fly from a lord not very filthy only, but very cruel and deceitful, which requireth so cruel service and so strait a task, which promiseth again things so uncertain, so caduke, so transitory, which so soon fade and vanish away, of the which very same things yet deceiveth he the wretches, and that not seldom. though he perform his promise once, yet another time when it pleaseth him he taketh them away again, so that the sorrow and thought for the loss of things once possessed is much more than was the grievous labour in purchasing them. that the merchant man hath mingled together both right and wrong for the intent of increasing his goods, after he hath put his honest reputation of good report that is sprung of him, his life, his soul in a thousand jeopardies, if it so be then that the chance of fortune hap aright at the latter end with all his travail, what other thing hath he prepared for himself more than the matter of miserable care if he keep his goods, if he lose them a perpetual torment? fortune chance amiss what remaineth but that he should be made twice a wretch wrapped in double misery, partly because he is disappointed of the thing whereon his hope hanged, beside that because he cannot remember so great labour spent in waste without much both sorrow of heart and grief of mind? No man enforceth with sure purpose to come to good living or conversation which hath not attained it. Christ as he is not mocked, so neither he mocketh any man. Remember another thing, when thou fliest out of the world unto Christ, if the world have any commodities or pleasures that thou forsakest them not, but changest trifles with things of more value. Who will not be very glad to change silver for gold, flint for precious stone? Thy friends be displeased? What then? thou shalt find more pleasant and better companions. Thou shalt lack outward pleasures of thy body, but thou shalt enjoy the inward pleasures of the mind, which be better, purer, and more certain. Thy goods must be diminished, nevertheless these riches increase which neither the moths destroy nor thieves take away. Thou ceasest to be of price in the world, but thou for all that art well beloved of Christ: thou pleasest the fewer, but yet the better. Thy body waxeth lean, but thy mind waxeth fat. The beauty of thy skin vanisheth away, but the beauty of thy mind appeareth bright. And in like manner if thou shalt reckon all other things thou shalt perceive nothing not of all these apparent good things to be forsaken in this world, that is not recompensed largely with greater advantage and more excellent a great way. if there be any things which though they cannot be desired without vice, yet without vice may be possessed: of which kind of things is the good estimation of the people, favour of the commonalty, love or to be in conceit, authority, friends, honour due to virtue: for the most part it chanceth that all these things be given without searching for, to them that above all things seek the kingdom of heaven, which selfsame thing Christ promised and God performed to Salomon. Fortune for the most part followeth them that flieth from her, and flieth from them that follow her. Certainly whatsoever shall happen to them that love, nothing can be but prosperous unto whom loss is turned to advantage, torment, vexation or adversity to solace, rebukes to laud, punishment to pleasure, bitter things to sweetness, evil things to good. Doubtest thou then to enter in to this way and forsake that other way, seeing there is so unequal comparison, yea none at all, of God unto the devil, of hope to hope, of reward to reward, of labour to labour, of solace to solace.

The fourth rule

CHAPTER XII

BUT that thou mayst haste and make speed unto felicity with a more sure course, let this be unto thee the fourth rule, that thou have Christ alway in thy sight as the only mark of all thy living and conversation, unto whom only thou shouldst direct all thine enforcements, all thy pastimes and purposes, all thy rest and quietness, and also thy business. think thou not Christ to be a voice or sound without signification, but think him to be nothing else save charity, simplicity, or innocency, patience, cleanness, and shortly whatsoever Christ taught. Understand well also that the devil is none other thing but whatsoever calleth away from such things as Christ taught. directeth his journey to Christ which is carried to virtue only. And he becometh bond to the devil which giveth himself to vices. Let thine eye therefore be pure, and all thy body shall be bright and full of light. Let thine eye look unto Christ alone as unto only and very felicity, so that thou love nothing, marvel at nothing, desire nothing but either Christ or else for Christ. Also that thou hate nothing, abhor nothing, fly nothing, nothing avoid but only sin or else for sin's sake. By this means it will come to pass that whatsoever thou shalt do, whether thou sleep, whether thou wake, whether thou eat, whether thou drink, and to conclude that thy very sports and pastimes, yea (I will speak more boldly) that some vices of the lighter sort into which we fall now and then while we haste to virtue, all the whole shall grow and turn in thee unto a great heap of rewards. But and if thine eye shall not be pure, but look any otherward than unto Christ, yea though thou do certain things which be good or honest of themselves, yet shall they be unfruitful or peradventure very perilous and hurtful. For it is a great fault to do a good thing not well. And therefore that man that hasteth the strait way unto the mark of very felicity, whatsoever things shall come and meet him by the way, so far forth ought he either refuse or receive them, they either further or hinder his journey: of which things there be three orders or

three degrees. Certain things verily be of such manner filthy that they cannot
be honest, as to avenge wrong, to wish evil to another. things ought alway to
be had in hate, yea though thou shouldest have never so great advantage to
commit them, or never so great punishment if thou didst them not, for nothing can hurt a good man but filthiness only. Certain things on the other side
be in such manner honest that they cannot be filthy, of which kind be to will
or wish all men good, to help thy friends with honest means, hate vices, to
rejoice with virtuous communication. Certain things verily be indifferent or
between both, of their own nature neither good nor bad, honest nor filthy: as
health, beauty, strength, fecundity, cunning, and such other. Of this last kind
of things therefore nothing ought to be desired for itself, neither ought to be
usurped more or less, but as far forth as they make and be necessary to the
chief mark, I mean, to follow Christ's living. The very philosophers have
certain marks also imperfect and indifferent, in which a man ought not to
stand still nor tarry, which also a man may conveniently use, referring them to
a better purpose, and not to enjoy them and tarry upon them, putting his
whole felicity in them: notwithstanding those mean and indifferent things do
not all after one manner and equally either further or hinder them that be
going unto Christ, therefore they must be received or refused, after as each of
them is more or less of value unto thy purpose. helpeth more unto piety than
beauty or strength of body or riches: and though all learning may be applied to
Christ, yet some helpeth more compendiously than some. Of this end and
purpose, see thou measure the profitableness or unprofitableness of all mean
things. lovest learning, it is very well if thou do it for Christ's sake: but if thou
love it therefore only because thou wouldst know it, then makest thou a stop
and tarrying therefrom whence thou oughtest to have made a step to climb
further. But if thou desire sciences that thou by their help mightest more
clearly behold Christ hid in the secrets of scripture, and when thou knowest
him love him, when thou knowest and lovest him teach, declare, and open him
to other men, and in thyself enjoy him: then prepare thyself unto study of
sciences, but no further than thou mayst think them profitable to good living.
If thou have confidence in thyself and trust to have great adavntage in Christ,
forth boldly as an adventurous merchant to walk as a stranger somewhat
further, yea in the learning of gentiles, and apply the riches or treasure of the
Egyptians unto the honesting of the temple of God. But if thou fear greater
loss than thou hopest of advantage, then return again to our first rule: know
thyself and pass not thy bounds, keep thee within thy lists. It is better to have
less knowledge and more of love, than to have more of knowledge and not to
love. Knowledge therefore hath the mastery or chief room amongst mean

things. After that is health, the gifts of nature, eloquence, beauty, strength, dignity, favour, authority, prosperity, good reputation, kin, friends, stuff of household. Every one of these things as it helpeth most and nighest way unto virtue, so shall it most chiefly be applied in case they be offered unto us hasting in our way, if not then may we not for cause of them turn aside from our journey purposed. chanced unto thee, if it let nothing to good living, minister it, make friends with the wicked mammon: but if thou fear loss of virtue and good mind, despise that advantage full of damage and loss, and follow thou even Crates of Thebes flinging thy grievous and cumbrous pack into the sea, than it should hold thee back from Christ. That thing mayst thou do the easier, if, as I have said, thou shalt custom thyself to marvel at none of those things which be without thee, that is to say, which pertain not unto the inner man, for by that means it will come to pass that thou canst neither wax proud or forget thyself. If these things fortune unto thee, neither thou shalt be vexed in thy mind if they should either be denied thee or taken from thee, forasmuch as thou puttest thy whole felicity in Christ only. But and if it chance they come unto thee besides thine own labour, be more diligent and circumspect, having no less care than thou hadst before: have in mind that a matter to exercise thyself virtuously on, is given to thee of God, but yet not without jeopardy and danger. if thou have the benignity of fortune suspected, counterfeit Prometheus, do not receive the deceitful box, and go light and naked unto that which is only very felicity. Certainly whosoever with great thought and care desire money as a precious thing, and count the chief succour of life to be therein, thinking themselves happy as long as it is safe, calling themselves wretches when it is lost: those men no doubt have made or feigned unto themselves many gods. Thou hast set up thy money and made it equal unto Christ, if it can make thee happy or unhappy. That I have spoken of money understand the same likewise of honours, voluptuousness, health, yea and of the very life of the body. We must enforce to come to our only mark, which is Christ, so fervently that we should have no leisure to care for any of these things, either when they be given us, or else when they be taken from us, for the time is short as saith Paul: Henceforward, saith he, they that use the world, must be as they used it not. This mind I know well the world laugheth to scorn as foolish and mad: nevertheless it pleaseth God by this foolishness to save them that believe. And the foolishness of God is wiser than man. After this rule thou shalt examine, yea whatsoever thou doest. Thou exercisest a craft? It is very well done if thou do it without fraud: but whereunto lookest thou to find thy household? But for what intent to find thy household, to win thy household to Christ? Thou runnest well. fastest, verily a good work as it appeareth outward: but unto what end referrest thou thyself, spare thy victuals or that thou mayst be counted the more holy? Thine eye is wanton, corrupt, and not pure. Peradventure thou fastest lest thou should fall into some disease or sickness. Why fearest thou sickness? Lest it would take thee from the use of voluptuous pleasures: thine eye is corrupt. But thou desireth health because thou mayst be able to study. To what purpose I beseech thee referrest thou thy study, to get thee a benefice withal? With what mind desirest thou a benefice? Verily to live at thine own pleasure, not at Christ's. Thou hast missed the mark which a christian man ought to have every where prefixed before his eyes. Thou takest meat that thou mightest be strong in thy body, and thou wilt have thy body strong that thou mightest be sufficient unto holy exercises and watch. Thou hast hit the mark. But thou providest for health and good living lest thou shouldest be more evil favoured or deformed, lest thou shouldst not be strong enough unto bodily lust, thou hast fallen from Christ making unto thee another God. be which honour certain saints with certain ceremonies. One saluteth Christofer every day, but not except he behold his image. looketh he? Verily to this point, he hath borne himself in hand that he shall be all that day sure from evil death. Another worshippeth one Rochus, but why? he believeth that he will keep away the pestilence from his body. mumbleth certain prayers to Barbara or George, lest he should fall into his enemy's hands. man fasteth to Saint Apolyne lest his teeth should ache. man visiteth the image of holy Job, he should be without scabs. Some assign and name certain portion of their winning to poor men, lest their merchandise should perish by shipwreck. taper is light before Saint Hierom to the intent that thing which is lost may be had again. In conclusion after this same manner look how many things be which we either favour or else love, so many saints have we made governors of the same things, which same saints be divers in divers natures: so that Paul doth the same thing among the Frenchmen that Hieron doth with our countrymen the Almayns, and neither James nor John can do that thing in everywhere which they do in this or that place: which honouring of saints truly, except it be referred from the respect of corporal commodities or incommodities unto Christ, is not for a christian man, insomuch that it is not far from the superstitiousness of them which in time past vowed the tenth part of their goods to Hercules, to the intent they might wax rich, a cock to Esculapius that they might be recovered of their diseases: which sacrificed a bull to Neptunus that they might have good passage by sea and prosperous sailing. The names be changed, but verily they have both one end and intent. prayest God that thou mayst not die too soon, or while thou art young, and prayest not rather that he would give to thee a good mind that in whatsoever place death should come upon thee he should not find thee unprepared. Thou thinkest not of changing thy life, and prayest God thou mightest not die. What prayest thou for then? Certainly that thou mightest sin as long as is possible. Thou desireth riches and cannot use riches, doest not thou then desire thine own confusion? Thou desirest health and canst not use health, is not now thy honouring of God dishonouring of God? In this place I am sure some of our holy men will cry out against me with open mouths, which think lucre to be to the honouring of God, and as the same Paul saith, with certain sweet benedictions deceive the minds of innocent persons while they obey and serve their belly and not Jesu Christ. Then will they say, forbiddest thou worship of saints in whom God is honoured? I verily dispraise not them so greatly which do those things with certain simple and childish superstition for lack of instruction or capacity of wit, I do them which seeking their own advantage prayeth and magnifieth those things for most great and perfect holiness, which things peradventure be tolerable and may be suffered, and for their own profit and advantage cherish and maintain the ignorance of the people, which neither I myself do despise, but I cannot suffer that they should account things to be highest and most chief, which of themselves be neither good nor bad, and those things to be greatest and of most value which be smallest and of least value. I will praise it and be content that they desire health of Rochus whom they so greatly honour, if they consecrate it unto Christ. But I will praise it more if they would pray for nothing else but that with the hate of vices the love of virtues might be increased: and as touching to live or to die let them put it into the hands of God, and let them say with Paul, whether we live, whether we die, to God and at God's pleasure we live or die. It shall be a perfect thing if they desire to be dissolved from, the body and to be with Christ: if they put their glory and joy in diseases or sickness, in loss or other damages of fortune, that they might be accounted worthy, which even in this world should be like or conformable unto their head. To do therefore such manner of things is not so much to be rebuked as it is perilous to abide still and cleave to them. I suffer infirmity and weakness, but with Paul I show a more excellent way. If thou shalt examine thy studies and all thy acts by this rule, and shalt not stand anywhere in mean things till thou come even unto Christ, thou shalt neither go out of thy way at any time, neither shalt do or suffer any thing in all thy life which shall not turn and be unto thee a matter of serving and honouring God.

The fifth rule

CHAPTER XIII

LET us add also the fifth rule as an aider unto this foresaid fourth rule, that thou put perfect piety, that is to say the honouring of God, in this thing only, if thou shalt enforce alway from things visible, which almost every one be imperfect or else indifferent to ascend to things invisible after the division of a man above rehearsed. This precept is appertaining to the matter so necessarily, that whether it be through negligence or for lack of knowledge of it, the most part of christian men instead of true honourers of God are but plain superstitious, and in all other things save in the name of christian men only, vary not greatly from the superstition of the gentiles. us imagine therefore two worlds, the one intelligible the other visible. The intelligible which also we may call the angelical world, wherein God is with blessed minds. The visible world, the circle of heaven, the planets, and stars, with all that included is in them as the four elements. Then let us imagine man as a certain third world, partaker of both the other: of the visible world if thou behold his body, of the invisible world if thou consider his soul. In the visible world because we be but strangers we ought never rest, but what thing soever offereth itself to the sensible powers, that is to say to the five wits, that must we under a certain apt comparison or similitude apply to the angelical world, or else (which is most profitable) unto manners and to that part of man which is correspondent to the angelic world, that is to say to the soul of man. this visible sun is in the visible world that is the divine mind, that is to say God, in the intelligible world, and in that part of thee which is of that same nature, that is to say in the spirit. Look what the moon is in the visible world, that in the invisible world is the congregation of angels and of blessed souls called the triumphant church, and that in thee is the spirit. Whatsoever heavens above worketh in the earth under them, that same doth God in the soul. The sun goeth down, ariseth, rageth in heat, is temperate, quickeneth, bringeth forth, maketh ripe, draweth to him, maketh subtle and thin, purgeth, hardeneth, mollifieth, illumineth, cleareth, cherisheth and comforteth. Therefore whatsoever thou beholdest in him, yea whatsoever thou seest in the gross part of this world of the elements which many have separated from the heavens above and circles of the firmament, in conclusion whatsoever thou considerest in the grosser part of thyself, accustom to apply it to God and to the invisible portion of thyself. So shall it come to pass that whatsoever thing shall anywhere offer itself to any of the sensible wits, that same thing shall be to thee an occasion of piety, to honour God. it delighteth thy corporal eyes as oft as this visible sun spreadeth himself on the earth with new light, by and by call to remembrance how great the pleasure is of the inhabitants of heaven, unto whom the eternal sun ever springeth and ariseth, but never goeth down. How great are the joys of that pure mind whereupon the light of God always shineth and casteth his beams. by occasion of the visible creature pray with the words of Paul, that he which commanded light to shine out of darkness may shine in thy heart, to give light and knowledge of the glory of God in the face of Jesu Christ. Repeat such like places of holy scripture in which here and there the grace of the spirit of God is compared to light. night seemeth tedious to thee and dark, think on a soul destitute of the light of God and dark with vices: yea and if thou canst perceive any darkness of night in thee, pray that the sun of justice may arise unto thee. This wise think and surely believe that things invisible which thou seest not are so excellent, so pure, so perfect, that things which be seen in comparison of them are scarce very shadows representing to the eyes a small and a thin similitude of them. Therefore in this outward corporal things what soever thy sensible wits either desire or abhor, it shall be a great deal meeter that the spirit love or hate the same thing in inward and incorporal things. goodly beauty of thy body pleaseth thine eyes, think then how honest a thing is the beauty of the soul. A deformed visage seemeth an unpleasant thing, remember how odious a thing is a mind defiled with vices: and of all other thine do likewise. For as the soul hath certain beauty wherewith one while she pleaseth God, and a deformity wherewith another while she pleaseth the devil, as like unto like: so hath she also her youth, her age, sickness, health, death, life, poverty, riches, joy, sorrow, war, peace, cold, heat, thirst, drink, hunger, meat. To conclude shortly, whatsoever is filthy in the body, that same is to be understood in the soul. Therefore in this thing resteth the journey to the spiritual and pure life, if by a little and little we shall accustom to withdraw ourself from these things which be not truly in very deed, partly appear to be that they be not: as filthy and voluptuous pleasure, honour of this world, partly vanish away and haste to return to naught, and shall be ravished and carried to these things which indeed are eternal, immutable and pure: which thing Socrates saw full well, a philosopher not so much in tongue and words as in living and deeds, for he saith that so only shall the soul depart happily from her body at the last end, if aforehand she have diligently through true knowledge recorded and practised death, and also have long time before by the despising of things corporal, and by the contemplation and loving of things spiritual, used herself to be as it were in a manner absent from the body. the cross unto which Christ calleth and exhorteth us, neither that death in which Paul willeth us to die with our head, as also the prophet saith: for thy sake we be slain all the day long, we be accounted as sheep appointed to be killed: neither that which the apostle writeth in other terms saying, seek those things that be above, not which be on the earth. Taste and have perceivance of things above, meaneth it any other thing than that we unto things corporal should be dull and made as though we were insensible and utterly without capacity? So that the less feeling we have in things of the body, so much the more sweetness we might find in things pertaining to the spirit, and might begin to live so much the trulier inwardly in the spirit, the less we lived outwardly in the body. In conclusion to speak more plainly, so much the less should move us things caduke and transitory, the more acquainted we were with things eternal. So much the less should we regard the shadows of things, the more we have begun to look up upon the very true things. This rule therefore must be had ever ready at hand, that we in no wise stand still anywhere in temporal things, but that we rise thence making as it were a step unto the love of spiritual things by matching the one with the other, or else in comparison of things which are invisible that we begin to despise that which is visible. The disease of thy body will be the easier if thou wouldest think it to be a remedy for thy soul. Thou shouldest care the less for the health of thy body if thou wouldest turn all thy care to defend and maintain the health of the mind. The death of the body putteth thee in fear, the death of the soul is much more to be feared. Thou abhorrest the poison which thou seest with thine eyes, because it bringeth mischief to the body: much more is the poison to be abhorred which slayeth the soul. is poison of the body, but voluptuousness is much more and ready poison to the soul. Thou quakest and tremblest for fear, thy hair standeth upright, thou art speechless, thy spirits forsake thee and thou waxest pale, fearing lest the lightning which appeareth out of the clouds should smite thee, but how much more is it to be feared lest there should come on thee the invisible lightning of the wrath of God, which saith: Go ye cursed persons into eternal fire? The beauty of the body ravisheth thee, why rather lovest thou not fervently that fairness that is not seen? Translate thy love into that beauty that is perpetual, that is celestial, that is without corruption, and the discreetlier shalt thou love the caduke and transitory shape of the body. Thou prayest that thy field may be watered with rain lest it dry up, pray rather that God will vouchsafe to water thy mind lest it wax barren from the fruit of virtues. restorest and increasest again with great care the waste of thy money: the greatest care of all oughtest thou have to restore again the loss of the mind. Thou hast a respect long aforehand to age, lest anything should be lacking to thy body: shouldest thou not provide that nothing be lacking to the mind? And this verily ought to be done in those things which daily meeteth our sensible wits, and as everything is of a diverse kind, even so diversely doth move us with hope, fear, love, hate, sorrow and joy. The same thing must be observed and kept in all manner of learning which include in themselves a plain sense and a mystery, even as they were made of a body and a soul, that the literal sense little regarded thou shouldest look chiefly to the mystery. Of which manner are the letters of all poets and philosophers, chiefly the followers of Plato. But most of all, holy scripture, which being in a manner like to Silenus of Alcibiades, under a rude and foolish covering include pure divine and godly things: for else if thou shalt read without the allegory the image of Adam formed of moist clay and the soul breathed into him, and Eve plucked out of the rib, how they were forbid the tree of knowledge of good and evil, the serpent enticing to eat, God walking at the air: when they knew they had sinned, how they hid themselves, the angel set at the doors with a turning sword lest after they were ejected, the way to them should be open to come again shortly: if thou shouldest read the whole history of the making of the world, if thou read (I say) superficially these things, seeking no further than appeareth outwardly, I cannot perceive what other great thing thou shalt do than if thou shouldest sing of the image of clay made by Prometheus, of fire stolen from heaven by subtlety and put into the image to give life to the clay. peradventure a poet's fable in the allegory shall be read with somewhat more fruit than a narration of holy books, if thou rest in the rind or outer part. If when thou readest the fable of the giants, it warneth and putteth thee in remembrance that thou strive not with God and things more mighty than thou, or that thou oughtest to abstain from such studies as nature abhorreth, and that thou shouldest set thy mind unto these things (if so be they be honest) whereunto thou art most apt naturally. That thou tangle not thyself with matrimony, if chastity be more agreeable to thy manners. Again that thou bind not thyself to chastity if thou seem more apt to marriage: most commonly those things come evil to pass which thou provest against nature. If the cup of Circe teach that men with voluptuousness as with witchcraft fall out of their mind and be changed utterly from men unto beasts. thirsty Tantalus teach thee that it is a very miserable thing for a man to sit gaping upon his riches heaped together and dare not use them. stone of Sisyphus, that ambition is laborious and miserable. the labours of Hercules putteth thee in remembrance that heaven must be obtained with honest labours and enforcements indefatigable: learnest thou not that thing in the fable which the philosophers teach and also divines, masters of good living? if (without allegory) thou shalt read the infants wrestling in their mother's belly, the inheritance of the elder brother sold for a mess of pottage, the blessing of the father prevented and taken away by fraud, Goly smitten with the sling of David, and the hair of Sampson shaven: is not of so great value as if thou shouldest read the feigning of some poet. What difference is there whether thou read the book of Kings or of the Judges in the Old Testament, or else the history of Titus Livyus, so thou have respect to the allegory nere nother? For in the one, that is to say Titus Livyus, be many things which would amend the common manners: in the other be some things, yea, ungoodly as they seem at the first looking on, which also if they be understood superficially should hurt good manners: the theft of David, and adultery bought with homicide, how the daughters of Lot lay with their father by stealth, and conceived, and a thousand other like matters. Therefore the flesh of the scripture despised chiefly of the Old Testament, it shall be meet and convenient to search out the mystery of the spirit. Manna to thee shall have such taste as thou bringest with thee in thy mouth. in opening of mysteries thou mayst not follow the conjectures of thine own mind, but the rule must be known and a certain craft, which one Dionisius teacheth in a book entitled De divinis nominibus, that is to say, of the names of God: and Saint Augustyne in a certain work called Doctrina christiana, that is to say, the doctrine of a christian man. apostle Paul after Christ opened certain fountains of allegory, whom Origene followed, and in that part of divinity obtained doubtless the chief room and mastery. our divines either set naught by the allegory or handle it very dreamingly and unfruitfully: yet are they in subtlety of disputation equal or rather superiors to old divines. But in treating of this craft that is to say in pure, apt, and fruitful handling, the allegory not once to be compared with them, and that specially as I guess for two causes. The one, that the mystery can be but weak and barren that is not fortified with strength of eloquence, and tempered with certain sweetness of speaking, in which our elders were passing excellent, and we not once taste of it. cause is, for they content with Arystotle only, expel from schools the sect of Plato and Pictagoras, and yet Saint Augustyn preferreth these latter, not only because they have many sentences much agreeable to our religion, but also because the very manner of open and clear speech, which they use (as I have said before) full of allegories, draweth very nigh to the style of holy scripture. marvel therefore though they have more commodiously handled the allegories of the word of God, which with plenteous oration were able to increase and dilate to colour and garnish any manner thing never so barren, simple, or homely, which men also being most expert and cunning of all antiquity had practised and exercised long before in poets and books of Plato, that thing which they should do after in divine mysteries. I had liefer that thou shouldest read the commentaries of those men, for I would instruct and induce thee not unto contention of arguments, but rather unto a pure mind. But and if thou cannot attain the mystery, remember yet that some thing lieth hid which though it be not known, yet verily to have trust to obtain it shall be better than to rest in the letter which killeth. And that see thou do not only in the Old Testament, but also in the New. The gospel hath her flesh, she hath also her spirit: though the veil be pulled from the face of Moses, nevertheless yet unto this day Paul saith per speculum in enigmate, not the thing itself and clearly, but the image or similitude of the very thing as it were in a glass imperfectly and obscurely: and as Christ himself sayeth in his gospel of John, The flesh profiteth nothing at all, it is the spirit that giveth life. I verily would have been afraid to have said it profiteth not at all, it should have been enough to say the flesh profiteth somewhat, but much more the spirit: but now verity himself hath said it profiteth not at all. And so greatly it profiteth not, that after the mind of Paul it is but death, except it be referred to the spirit: yet at the least way in this thing is the flesh profitable for that she leadeth our infirmity as it were with certain graces or steps unto the spirit. The body without the spirit can have no being: the spirit of the body hath no need. Wherefore if after the doctrine of Christ the spirit be so great and excellent a thing, that he only giveth life: hither to this point must our journey be, that in all manner letters, in all our acts, we have respect to the spirit, and not to the flesh. And if a man would take heed, he should soon perceive that this thing only is it whereunto exhorteth us among the prophets specially Esaias, among the apostles Paul, which almost in every epistle playeth this part and crieth that we should have no confidence in the flesh, and that in the spirit is life, liberty, light, adoption: those noble fruits so greatly to be desired which he numbereth.

The flesh everywhere he despiseth, condemneth, and counselleth from her. Take heed and thou shalt perceive that our master Christ doth the same thing here and there, whiles in pulling the ass out of the pit, in restoring the sight to the blind, in rubbing the ears of corn, in unwashen hands, in the feasts of sinners, in the parable of the pharisee and the publican, in fastings, in the carnal brethren, in the rejoicing of the Jews that they were the children of

Abraham, in offering of gifts in the temple, in praying, dilating of their phylac-
teries, and in many like places he despiseth the flesh of the law, and superstition of them which had liefer be Jews openly in the sight of man than privily
in the sight of God. And when he said to the woman of Samary, believe me
that the hour shall come when ye shall honour the father neither in this mountain, neither in Jerusalem: but the hour shall be and now is when the very true
worshippers shall worship the father in spirit and verity: for surely the father
requireth such to honour him: the father is a spirit, and they which honour
him must honour in spirit and verity. He signified the same thing indeed when
at the marriage he turned the water of the cold and unsavoury letter into wine
of the spirit, making drunk the spiritual souls, even unto the contempt and
despising of their life. And lest thou shouldest think it a great thing that Christ
despised these things which now I have rehearsed, yea he despised the eating of
his own flesh and drinking of his own blood, except it were done spiritually.
To whom thinkest thou spake he these things: The flesh profiteth nothing at
all, it is the spirit that quickeneth and giveth life? not to them which with Saint
John's gospel or an agnus dei hanging about their necks think themselves sure
from all manner of harm, and suppose that thing to be the very perfect religion
of a christian man: but to them to whom he opened the high mystery of eating
his own body. If so great a thing be of no value, yea if it be pernicious or
perilous: what cause is there wherefore we should have confidence in any other
carnal things except the spirit be present? Thou peradventure sayest mass daily
and livest at thine own pleasure, and art not once moved with thy neighbour's
hurts, no, no more than if they pertained nothing at all to thee: thou art yet in
the flesh of the sacrament: but and if while thou sayest, thou enforcest to be
the very same thing which is signified by receiving that sacrament, that is to
say, to be one spirit with the spirit of Christ, to be one body with the body of
Christ, to be a quick member of the church: if thou love nothing but in Christ,
if thou think all thy goods to be common to all men, if the incommodities of
all men grieve thee even as thine own: then no doubt thou sayest mass with
great fruit, and that because thou doest it spiritually. If thou perceive that thou
art in a manner transfigured and changed into Christ, and that thou livest now
less and less in thine own self, give thanks to the spirit which only quickeneth
and giveth life. Many been wont to number how many masses they have been
at every day, and having confidence in this thing as of most value (as though
now they were no farther bound to Christ) as soon as they be departed out of
the church return to their old manners again: that they embrace the flesh of
piety, that is to say of pure life or service of God I dispraise not: that they there
stop I praise not: let that be performed in thee which is there represented to

thine eyes. is represented to thee, the death of thy head: discuss thyself within-forth, and (as the saying is) in thy bosom, how nigh thou art dead to the world. For if thou be possessed wholly with wrath, ambition, covetousness, envy, yea though thou touch the altar, yet art thou far from mass. Christ was slain for thee, flee thou therefore these beasts, sacrifice thyself to him which for thy sake sacrificed himself to his father: if thou once think not on these things, and hast confidence in the other, God hateth thy carnal and gross religion. Thou art baptised, think not forthwith that thou art a christian man, thy mind altogether favoureth nothing but this world: thou art in the sight of the world a christian man, but secret and before God thou art more heathen than any heathen man. Why so? For thou hast the body of the sacrament and art with-out the spirit which only profiteth. Thy body is washed, what matter maketh that while thy mind remaineth still defiled and inquinate? Thy body is touched with salt, what then when thy mind is yet unsavoury? Thy body is anointed, but thy mind unanointed. But if thou be buried with Christ withinforth, and studiest to walk with him in the new life I then know thee for a christian man. art sprinkled with holy water, what good doth that, if so be thou wipe not away the inward filth from thy mind? honourest saints and art joyous and glad to touch their relics, but thou despiseth the chief relics which they left behind them, that is to be understood the examples of pure living. There is no honour more pleasant to Mary than if thou shouldest counterfeit her humility. religion is more acceptable to saints or more appropriate than if thou wouldest labour to represent and follow their virtues. Wilt thou deserve the love and favour of Peter or of Paul, counterfeit the one's faith, and the other's charity, and thou shalt do a greater thing than if thou shouldest run to Rome x. times. Wilt thou worship Saint Fraunces singularly? Thou art high minded, thou art a great lover of money, thou art stubborn and self-willed, full of contention, wise in thine own opinion, give this to the saint, assuage thy mind, and by the exam-ple of Saint Fraunces be more sober, humble or meek, despise filthy lucre, and be desirous of riches of the mind, put away striving and debates with thy neighbours and with goodness overcome evil. The saint setteth more by this honour than if thou shouldest set before him a thousand burning tapers. Thou thinkest it a special thing to be put in thy grave wrapped in the cowl or habit of Saint Fraunces? Trust me, like vesture shall profit thee nothing at all when thou art dead, if thy living and manners be found unlike when thou were alive. And though the sure example of all true virtue and pure life, shewing how thou shouldest honour God in everything, is set of Christ most commodiously in such manner, that in no wise thou canst be deceived. Nevertheless if the worshipping of Christ in his saints delight thee so greatly, see that thou counterfeit Christ in his saints, for the honour of every saint look thou put away all vices, vice by vice, so that thou sacrifice to every saint singularly some one vice singularly, or else study to embrace and counterfeit some one singular virtue in every saint, such as thou perceivest to have reigned most chiefly in every saint, singularly of them which thou worshippest so specially. If this shall come to pass, then will I not reprove those things which be done outwardly. Thou hast in great reverence the ashes of Paul, I damn it not, if thy religion be perfect in every point, but if thou have in reverence the dead ashes or powder of his body, and settest no store by his quick image yet speaking, and as it were breathing, which remaineth in his doctrine: is not thy religion preposterous and out of order and according to the common proverb, the cart set before the horse? thou the bones of Paul hid in the shrine, and honourest thou not the mind of Paul hid in his writings? Magnifiest thou a piece of his carcase shining through a glass, and regardest not thou the whole mind of Paul shining through his letters? Thou worshippest the ashes in whose presence now and then the deformities and diseases of bodies be taken away, why rather honourest thou not his doctrine, wherewith the deformities and diseases of souls are cured and remedied? Let the unfaithful marvel at these miracles and signs for whom they be wrought: but thou that art a faithful man embrace his books, that as thou doubtest not, but that God can do all things, even so thou mightest learn to love him above all things. honourest the image of the bodily countenance of Christ formed in stone or tree, or else portrayed with colours: with much greater reverence is to be honoured the image of his mind, which by workmanship of the Holy Ghost is figured and expressed in the gospels. any Apelles so expressly fashioned with pencil the proportions and figure of the body as in the oration and doctrine of every man appeareth the image of the mind, namely in Christ, which when he was very simplicity and pure verity, no discord, no unlike thing at all could be between the spirit and chief pattern of his divine mind and the image of his doctrine and learning from thence deduct and derivate, as nothing is more like the father of heaven than his son, which is the word, the wisdom and knowledge of the father, springing forth of his most secret heart: so is nothing more like unto Christ than the word, the doctrine and teaching of Christ, given forth out of the privy parts of his most holy breast: and ponderest thou not this image? Honourest it not? Lookest thou not substantially with devout eyes upon it? Embracest it not in thy heart? Hast thou of thy lord and master relics so holy, so full of virtue and strength, and setting them at nought, seekest thou things much more alienate, stranger and farther off? Thou beholdest a coat or a sudorye, that is said to have been Christ's, astonied thereat as though thy wits were rapt: and art thou in a dream or a slumber when thou readest the divine oracles or answers of Christ? Thou believest it to be a great thing, yea a greater than the greatest that thou possessest at home a little piece of the cross: that is nothing to be compared to this, if thou bear shrined in thy heart the mystery of the cross. Or else if such things make a man religious and devout, what can be more religious than the Jews, of which very many (though they were never so wicked) yet with their eyes saw Jesus Christ living bodily, heard him with their ears, with their hands handled him. What is more happy than Judas, which with his mouth kissed the divine mouth of Christ? So much doth the flesh without the spirit profit nothing at all, that it should not once have profited the holy virgin his mother that she of her own flesh begat him, except she in her spirit had conceived his spirit also: this is a very great thing, but hear a greater. The apostles enjoyed the corporal presence and fellowship of Christ (readest thou not) how weak, how childish they were, how gross and without capacity. would desire any other thing unto the most perfect health of his soul, than so long familiarity and conversation together with him that was both God and man? Yet after so many miracles shewed, after the doctrine of his own mouth taught and declared to them, after sure and evident tokens that he was risen again, did he not at the last hour when he should be received up into heaven cast in their teeth their unstability in the faith? What was then the cause? Verily the flesh of Christ did let: and thence it is that he saith: Except I go away, the Holy Ghost will not come, it is expedient for you that I depart. The corporal presence of Christ is unprofitable unto health. And dare we in any corporal thing beside that put perfect piety, that is to say, the love and honour of God? Paul saw Christ in his humanity, what supposest thou to be a greater thing than that? Yet setteth he nought by it, saying, though (saith he) we have known Christ carnally, now we do not so. Why knew he him not carnally? For he had profited and ascended unto more perfect gifts of the spirit. I use peradventure more words in disputing these things than should be meet for him which giveth rules: nevertheless I do it the more diligently (and not without a great cause) for that in very deed I do perceive this error to be the common pestilence of all christendom: which bringeth and occasioneth, yea for this causeth, the greater mischief: forasmuch as in semblance and appearance it is next unto godly love or holiness. For there are no vices more perilous than they which counterfeit virtue: for besides this that good men may lightly fall into them: none are with more difficulty cured, because the common people unlearned thinketh our religion to be violate when such things are rebuked: let incontinent all the world cry out against me, let certain preachers, such as are wont to cry out in their pulpits, bark which with right good will sing these things inwardly in their own stomachs looking verily not unto Christ, but unto their own advantage, through whose either superstition without learning, or feigned holiness, I am compelled oftentimes to shew and declare that I in no wise rebuke or check the corporal ceremonies of christian men and devout minds of simple persons: namely in such things that are approved by authority of the church. For they are now and then partly signs of piety and partly helpers thereunto. And because they are somewhat necessary to young infants in Christ, till they wax older and grow up unto a perfect man: it is not meet they should be disdained of them which are perfect, lest by their example the weak person should take harm. That thou doest I approve, so the end be not amiss. Moreover if thou stop not there whence thou oughtest to ascend to things more near to health: but to worship Christ with visible things instead of invisible and in them to put the highest point of religion, and for them to stand in thine own conceit, to condemn other men, to set thy whole mind upon them, and also to die in them, and to speak shortly that thou be withdrawn from Christ with the very same things which be ordained for the intent only that they should help unto Christ: this is verily to depart from the law of the gospel which is spiritual, and fall into certain superstition of ceremonies like unto the Jews: which thing peradventure is of no less jeopardy than if without such superstition thou shouldest be infect with great and manifest vices of the mind: this is forsooth the more deadly disease. Be it, but the other is worse to be cured. How much everywhere sweateth the chief defender of the spirit Paul to call away the Jews from the confidence of deeds and ceremonies, and to promote them unto those things which are spiritual: now I see the commonality of christian men to be returned hither again. But what said I the commonality? That might be yet suffered had not this error invaded and caught a great part both of priests and doctors: and to be short, the flocks of them almost throughout which profess in title and habit a spiritual life. If they which should be the very salt be unsavoury: wherewithal shall other be seasoned? am ashamed to rehearse with what superstition the most part of them observe certain ceremonies of men's inventions, yet not institute for such purpose. How odiously they require them of other men: what confidence without mistrust they have in them: how indifferently they judge other men: how earnestly they defend them. To these their deeds they think heaven to be due, in which if they be once rooted at once they think themselves Pauls and Antonys.

They begin, O good Lord, with what gravity, with how great authority, to correct other men's lives, after the rule of fools and indiscreet persons (as saith Terence), so that they think nothing well done but that they do themselves. for all that when they be waxen old sires in their manner of living thou shalt see that as yet they savour or taste of Christ nothing at all: but to be beastly swimming in certain churlish vices in their living and pastime froward, and scarce can suffer and forbear their own self: in charity cold: in wrath fervent: in hate as tough as white leather: in their tongues venemous and full of poison: in exercising and putting forth of their malice conquerors and not able to be overcome: ready to strive for every little trifle: and so far from the perfection of Christ, that they be not once endued with these common virtues, which the very ethnics or heathen men have learned, either by reason given to them of nature, or by use of living, or by the precepts of philosophers. Thou shalt also see them in spiritual things clean without capacity, fierce that no man shall know how to entreat or handle them, full of strife and contention, greedy upon voluptuous pleasure, at the word of God ready to spue, kind to no man, misdeeming other men, flattering their own selves. It is come to this point now at last with the labours of so many years, that thou shouldest be of all men the worst, and yet think thyself the best: that instead of a christian man thou shouldest be but a plain Jew, observing only unfruitful traditions and ceremonies of the inventions of man, that thou shouldest have thy glory and joy, not in secret before God, but openly afore the world. But and if thou hast walked in the spirit and not in the flesh: where be the fruits of the spirit? Where is charity? Where is that cheerfulness or joyous mirth of a pure mind? Where is tranquillity and peace towards all men? Where is patience? Where is perseverance of soft mind, wherewith thou lookest day by day continually for the amendment even of thine enemies? where is courtesy or gentleness, where is freeness of heart, where is meekness, fidelity, discretion, measure or soberness, temperance and chastity? where is the image of Christ in thy manners? I am, sayst thou, no keeper of whores, no thief, no violator of holy things, I keep my profession. But what other thing is this to say than I am not like other men, extortioners, adulterers, yea and I fast twice in a week? had liefer have a publican humble and lowly asking mercy than this kind of pharisees rehearsing their good deeds. But what is thy profession? is it I pray thee that thou shouldest not perform that thing thou promised long ago when thou wert baptised, which was that thou wouldest be a christian man, that is to say, a spiritual person, and not a carnal Jew, which for the traditions of man shouldest transgress the commandments of God? Is not the life of a christian man spiritual? Hear Paul speaking to the Romans. No damnation is to them that are grafted in Christ Jesu, which walk not carnally or after the flesh: for the law of the spirit of life in Christ Jesu hath delivered me from the law of sin and death: for that which the law weakened by reason of the flesh could not perform or make good, that same, God made good, sending his Son in the similitude of flesh prone to sin, and of sin condemned sin in the flesh, that the justifying of the law might be fulfilled in us which walk not after the flesh but after the spirit: for they that be in the flesh, be wise in things pertaining to the flesh: but they which be in the spirit perceive those things that pertain to the spirit: for they that be in the flesh, be wise in things pertaining to the flesh: but they which be in the spirit perceive those things that pertain to the spirit: for wisdom of the flesh is death, and wisdom of the spirit is life and peace: for the wisdom of the flesh is an enemy to God because she is not obedient to the law of God, nor yet can be. They that be in the flesh, they cannot please God: what could be spoken more largely? What more plainly? nevertheless many men subtle and crafty to flatter or favour their own vices: prone and ready without advisement to check other men's, think these things to pertain to themselves nothing at all: and that Paul spake of walking carnally or after the flesh, they refer to adulterers only and keepers of queans: that he spake of wisdom of the flesh which is enemy to God, they turned it to them which have learned humanity, or that they call secular sciences: in either other they set up their crests, and clap their hands for joy, both that they neither be adulterers, and in all sciences stark fools. Moreover to live in the spirit they dream to be none other thing than to do as they themselves do: which persons if they would as diligently observe the tongue of Paul as they maliciously despise Tully's, should soon perceive that the apostle calleth the flesh that thing that is visible and the spirit that thing that is invisible: for he teacheth everywhere that things visible ought to serve to things invisible: and not contrarywise invisible things to serve things visible. Thou of a preposterous order appliest Christ to those things which were meet to be applied unto Christ: requirest thou of me record that this word flesh pertaineth not only to filthy and superstitious lust of the body? Hold and understand that thing which the said apostle (doing that same which he in all places doth) writeth to the Colocenses. Let no man mislead you for the nonce in the humility and religion of angels which things he never saw, walking in vain, inflate with the imagination of the flesh, and not holding the head, that is to say Christ, of whom all the body by couples and joints ministered up and compact, groweth into the increase of God. And lest thou shouldest doubt any thing that he spake of them which having confidence in certain corporal ceremonies bark against the spiritual purposes of other men: take heed what followeth: If ye be dead with Christ, ab elementis hujus mundi, from traditions, ceremonies and inventions of men: why have ye yet such decrees among you, as though ye lived unto the world? And anon after calling us from the same things, saith: If ye be risen up again with Christ, seek those things that are above where Christ sitteth on the right hand of God. Be expert and wise in those things that be above, and not on the earth. Moreover giving precepts of the spiritual life, what exhorteth he us to do at last? whether that we should use such or such ceremonies: whether that we should be this or that wise arrayed, that we should live with this or that meats, that we should say customably any certain number of psalms? he made mention of no such things. What then? (said he) your members which be on the earth, fornication, uncleanness, bodily lust, evil concupiscence, and avarice which is the service of idols: and a little after, that now put from you all such things, wrath, indignation, malice: and again, spoiling yourself of the old man with all his acts putting on you the new man which is renewed in knowledge of God after the image of him which made him. But who is the old man? Adam, he that was made of the earth, whose conversation is in earth, not in heaven. By the earth understand whatsoever is visible, and therefore temporal and transitory. Who is that new man? Verily the celestial man that descended from heaven, Christ. And by heaven understand whatsoever is invisible, and therefore eternal and everlasting. At the last, lest we should be minded to purchase the favour of God after the manner of the Jews with certain observances, as ceremonies magical, he teacheth that our deeds are pleasant and allowed of God, so long as they are referred unto charity, and also spring thereof, saying: Above all these things keep charity the bond of perfection, and let the peace of God rejoice as a victor in your hearts, in which also ye be called in one body. I will give thee a more plain token and evident probation that this word flesh signifieth not the lust of the body only. Paul nameth often the flesh, often the spirit, writing to a certain people named Galatas, which he called not only from lust of the body to chaste living but enforceth to withdraw them from the sect of the Jews and confidence of work into which they were induced by false apostles. In this place therefore numbering the deeds of the flesh, mark what vices he rehearseth. The deeds of the flesh (saith he) be manifest, which are fornication, uncleanness, to be shameless, lechery, worshipping of idols, witchcraft, privy hate, discord, otherwise called contention or strife, emulation that may be called indignation or disdain, ire otherwise called wrath, scolding dissension, that is to say, diversity in maintaining of opinions, sects, or maintaining of quarrels, envy, homicide, drunkenness, excess in eating, and such like. And not long after he saith: If we live in the spirit, let us walk in the spirit. After that as declaring and uttering a pestilence contrary to the spirit, he addeth: us not be made desirous of vainglory, provoking one the other, and envying one another. The tree is known by the fruit. That thou omittest not watch, fasting, silence, orisons, and such other like observances, I pass not thereon, I will not believe that thou art in the spirit except I may see the fruits of the spirit. Why may I not affirm thee to be in the flesh when after almost a hundred years exercise of these things, yet in thee I find the deeds of the flesh, enviousness more than is in any woman, continual wrath and fierceness as in a man of war, scolding, lust and pleasure insatiable, malicious cursing, backbiting with tongue more venemous than the poison of a serpent, an high mind, stubbornness, light of thy promise, vanity, feigning, flattering? Thou judgest thy brother in his meat, drink or raiment, but Paul judgeth thee of thy deeds. Doth that separate thee from worldly and carnal men, that thou art in lighter causes verily but yet with the same vices infected? is he more filthy, which, for his inheritance taken from him or it came to his hands, for his daughter defiled, for hurt done to his father, for some office, for his prince's favour: conceiveth wrath, hatred, emulation (which may be called indignation or disdain), than thou which (I am ashamed to tell) for how little a trifle, yea for nothing, doest all the same things much more maliciously, the lighter occasion to sin lighteneth not, but aggravateth the sin, neither it maketh matter in how little or great a thing thou sin, so it be done with like affection: and yet is there difference verily: for so much the grievouser doth every man trespass, the less the occasion is wherewith he is pulled away from honesty. speak not now of those monks or religious persons whose manners even the whole world abhorreth, but of them whom the common people honoureth not as men, but as angels, which selfsame notwithstanding ought not to be displeased with these words, which rebuketh the vices and noteth not the persons: but and if they be good men, let them also be glad to be warned of whatsoever man it be, in those things which pertaineth to health: neither it is unknown to me that amongst them are very many which holpen with learning and wit have tasted the mysteries of the spirit, (but as Livius saith) it fortuneth almost every where, that the greater part overcometh the better. Notwithstanding (if it be lawful to confess the truth) see we not all the most strait kind of monks to put the chief point of religion either in ceremonies or in a certain manner or form of saying, that they call their divine service, or in a labour of the body, which monks if a man should examine and appose of spiritual things, he should scarce find any at all that walked not in the flesh. And hereof cometh this so great infirmity of minds, trembling for fear where is no fear, and therein surety and careless where is most peril of all: hereof cometh the perpetual infancy in Christ (to speak no more grievously) that the preposterous esteemers of things make most of such things which by themselves are of no value: set at nought which only are sufficient, ever living under tutors or schoolmasters, ever in bondage, never advancing ourselves up to the liberty of the spirit, never growing up to the large stature of charity: when Paul crieth to a certain people called Galathas, Stand fast, be not ye locked again under the yoke of bondage. And in another place the law was our tutor or schoolmaster in Christ, that of faith we should be justified. But seeing that faith is come, now we be no more under a tutor or schoolmaster: for every one of you (saith he) is the very son of God through faith which he hath in Christ Jesu. And not much after he saith, And we also when we were little ones were in service and bondage under the ceremonies and law of this world. But when the time was fully expired, God sent his Son made of a woman, made under the law, to redeem them which were under the law, that we by adoption should be his sons. And for because ye be the sons of God, God hath sent the spirit of his Son into your hearts, crying, Abba, pater (as a man would say, Dada, father). And so is he not now a servant but a son to God. And again in another place: Brethren ye be called into liberty, let not your liberty be an occasion unto you to live in the flesh, but in charity of the spirit serve one another: for all the law is fulfilled in one saying: Love thy neighbour as thyself, but and if ye bite and eat one the other, take heed lest ye be consumed one of another. And again, to the Romans: Ye have not received the spirit of bondage again in fear, but the spirit that maketh you the sons of God by adoption, in whom we cry, Dada, father. Unto the same also pertaineth that he writeth to Timothy, saying: Exercise thyself under the deeds of piety: for bodily exercise is good but for a small thing, piety is good unto all manner things. And to the Corynthes: God is a spirit, and where the spirit is, there is liberty. But why rehearse I one or two places, when Paul is altogether at this point, that the flesh which is full of contention should be despised, and that he might settle us in the spirit which is the author of charity and liberty. For these companions be ever inseparable, on the one side, the flesh, bondage, unquietness, contention or strife: and on the other side, the spirit, peace, love, liberty. These things everywhere Paul mingleth with other sayings. And seek we a better master of our religion, namely when all divine scripture agreeth to him? This was the greatest commandment in the law of Moses. This Christ iterateth and finisheth in the gospel: and for this cause chiefly was he born: for this cause died he, to teach us not to counterfeit the Jews, but to love. the last supper made the even before his passion, how diligently, how tenderly, and how affectionately gave he charge to his disciples, not of meat, not of drink, of charity to be kept one towards another: what other thing teacheth he, what other thing desireth his disciple John, than that we love one another? Paul everywhere (as I have said) commendeth charity, but specially writing unto the Corynthes he preferreth charity both before miracles and prophecies, and also before the tongues of angels. And say not thou by and by that charity is, to be oft at the church, to crouch down before the images of saints, to light tapers or wax candles, to say many lady psalters or Saint Katheryne's knots. God hath no need of these things. calleth charity to edify thy neighbour, to count that we all be members of one body, to think that we all are but one in Christ, to rejoice in God of thy neighbour's wealth even as thou doest of thine own, to remedy his incommodities or losses as thine own. If any brother err or go out of the right way, to warn him, to admonish him, to tell him his fault meekly, soberly and courteously: to teach the ignorant: to lift up him that is fallen: to comfort and courage him that is in heaviness: to help him that laboureth: to succour the needy.

In conclusion to refer all riches and substance, all thy study, all thy cares to this point, that thou in Christ shouldest help as much as thy power extendeth to. That as he neither was born for himself, nor lived to his own pleasure, neither died for himself but dedicate himself wholly to our profits: even so should we apply ourselves, and await upon the commodities of our brethren, and not our own: which thing if it were used, nothing should be either more pleasant or else easy than the life of religious persons, which we see now clean contrary, almost everywhere and laborious, and also full of superstition, like unto the Jews, neither pure from any vices of the lay people, and in many sundry things much more defiled, kind of men Saint Augustyne (of whom many glory and rejoice as of the author and founder of their living) if he now might live again, certainly would not once know, and would cry out, saying that he would approve nothing less than this kind of life, and that he had instituted an order and manner of living, not after the superstition of the Jews, but after the rule of the apostles. But I hear even now what certain men (which are somewhat well advised) will answer unto me. A man must take heed in little and small things, lest a little and a little he should fall into greater vices, I hear it right well, and I allow the saying, nevertheless thou oughtest to take heed a great deal more that thou so cleave not to these little and small things that thou shouldest fall clean from the most chief and greatest things. is the jeopardy more evident, but here more grievous. flee Scylla that thou fall not into Charybdis. observe these little things is wholesome verily: but to cleave utterly unto them is very jeopardous. Paul forbiddeth not thee to use the law and ceremonies, but he will not him to be bound to the law and ceremonies which is free in Christ: he condemneth not the law of deeds, if a man use it lawfully: without these things peradventure thou shalt not be a christian man, but they make thee not a christian man, they will help unto piety and godliness, even so yet if thou use them for that purpose. and if thou shalt begin to enjoy them, to put thy trust and confidence in them, at once they utterly destroy all the living of a christian man. The apostle setteth nought by the deeds of Abraham, which to have been very perfect no man doubteth: hast thou confidence in thine? God disdaineth certain sacrifices called victim, the sabbotes and certain holy days called Neomenye of his people the Jews, of which things he himself was author and commander, and darest thou compare thine own observances with the precepts of the law of God? yet hear God ready to spue at them and aggrieved with them. what intent (saith he) offer ye to me the multitude of victims, I am full. As for holocausts of wethers, tallow or inward suet and fat of beasts, blood of calves, of lambs and goats, I would not have, when ye come before my presence, hath required these things of your hands that ye might walk in my houses? Offer ye no more sacrifice in vain, your incense is abomination to me, I will not suffer any more the feast of the Neomenye and sabbath day, with other feast days. companies of you are infected with iniquity, my soul hath hated your kalendas and your solemn feasts. These things be grievous unto me, I was even sick to abide them. when ye put forth your hands, I will turn mine eyes from you, when ye rehearse the observances and manners of holy feasts and sacrifice: moreover the multiplying of prayers, noteth he not them as though he pointed them with his finger, which measure their religion with a certain number of psalms and prayers, which they call daily service. Mark also another thing, how marvellously the facundyous prophet expresseth heaping together the disdain or indignation of God: that he now could suffer neither with ears, neither eyes. What things (I beseech thee)? verily those things which he himself had ordained to be kept so religiously, which also were observed so reverently so many years of holy kings and prophets. And these things abhorreth he as yet in the carnal law. And trustest thou in ceremonies made at home in thine own house, now in the law of the spirit? God in another place biddeth the same prophet to cry incessantly and to put out his breast after the manner of a trump, as in an earnest matter and worthy to be rebuked sharply, and such a matter as unneth could be obtained of these men but with much ado. Me (saith he) they seek from day to day, and know they well my ways, as a people that hath done justice, and hath not forsaken the judgment of their God. They ask me for the judgments of justice, and desire to draw nigh to God: why have we fasted (say they) and thou hast not looked upon us and meeked our souls, and thou wouldest not know it: lo, in the day of your fast (answereth the prophet) your own will is found in you, and ye seek out all your debtors, lo, unto strife and contention ye fast, and ye smite with your fist cruelly, fast ye not as ye have fasted unto this day, that your cry might be heard on high. Is this the fast that I have chosen, that a man should vex and trouble himself for one day, either that a man should bow down his head as a hook or circle, and to straw underneath him sackcloth and ashes? wilt thou call this a fast or a day acceptable unto

God? But what shall we say this to be? doth God condemn that thing, which
he himself commanded? Nay, forsooth. What then? but to cleave and stick fast
in the flesh of the law, and to have confidence of a thing of nothing, that is it
verily which he hateth deadly. Therefore he sheweth that he would have added
in either place. Be ye washed (said he) and made clean, take away your evil
cogitations and thoughts out of my sight. When thou hearest the evil thoughts
rehearsed, toucheth he not evidently the spirit and the inward man? The eyes
of God seeth not outward, but in secret, neither he judgeth after the sight of
the eyes, neither rebuketh after the hearing of the ears. God knoweth not the
foolish virgins, smooth and gay outward, empty of good works inward: he
knoweth not them which say with lips, Master, master. he putteth us in remembrance that the use of the spiritual life standeth not so greatly in ceremonies as in the charity of thy neighbour. Seek (saith he) judgment or justice,
succour him that is oppressed, give true judgment and right to him that is
fatherless and motherless or friendless, defend the widow. Such like things did
he knit to the other place, where he speaketh of fasting. Is not this rather (saith
he) that fast I have chosen: or cancel cruel obligations, unbind the burdens
which make them stoop to the ground that bear them: let them that be bruised
go free and break asunder all burden: break thy bread to hungry. The needy
and them which hath no place of habitation, lead in to thy house. When thou
seest a naked man clothe him, and despise not thine own flesh. What shall a
christian man do then? Shall he despise the commandments of the church?
Shall he set at naught the honest traditions of forefathers? he condemn godly
and holy customs? Nay, if he be weak and as a beginner he shall observe them
as things necessary, but and if he be strong and perfect so much the rather shall
he observe them, lest with his knowledge he should hurt his brother which is
yet weak, lest he also should kill him for whom Christ died: we may not omit
these things, but of necessity we must do other things. Corporal deeds be not
condemned, but spiritual are preferred. This visible honouring of God is not
condemned, but God is not pleased saving with invisible piety and service.
God is a spirit and is moved and stirred with invisible sacrifice. It is a great
shame for christian men not to know that thing which a certain poet being a
gentile knew right well, which giving a precept of due serving God, saith: If
God be a mind as scripture sheweth us, see that thou honour him chiefly with
a pure mind. Let us not despise the author being either an heathen man or
without degree of school, the sentence becometh yea a right great divine: and
(as I very well have perceived) is likewise understood of few as it is read of
many. The intellection of the sentence verily is this, like rejoysen with like.
Thou thinkest God to be moved greatly with an ox killed and sacrificed, or

with the vapour or smoke of frankincense, as though he were a body. God is a mind, and verily mind most pure, most subtle and perfect, therefore ought he to be honoured most chiefly with a pure mind. Thou thinkest that a taper lighted is sacrifice, but a sacrifice to God (saith David) is a woeful or sorrowful spirit. though he hath despised the blood of goats and calves, yet will he not despise a heart contrite and humble. If thou do that thing which is given to the eyes of men, much rather take heed that thing not to be away which the eyes of God require. Thy body is covered with a cowl or habit: what is that to the purpose if thy mind bear a secular vesture? If thy outer man be cloaked in a cloak white as snow, let the vestments of thy inner man be white as snow also, agreeable to the same. Thou keepest silence outward, much more procure that thy mind be quiet within. In the visible temple thou bowest down the knees of thy body: that is nothing worthy if in the temple of thy breast thou stand upright against God. Thou honourest the tree of the cross, much more follow the mystery of the cross. Thou keepest the fasting day and abstainest from those things which defile not a man: and why abstainest thou not from filthy talking, which polluteth thine own conscience and other men's also? Meat is withdrawn from the body, but why glutteth thy soul herself with cods of beans, pease, and such like which are meat meet for swine? Thou makest the church of stone gay with goodly ornaments, thou honourest holy places: what is it to the purpose if the temple of thy heart, whose walls the prophet Ezechyell bored through, be profaned or polluted with the abominations of Egypt? keepest the sabbath day outward, and within all things be unquiet through the rage and tumbling of vices together. Thy body committeth no adultery, but thou art covetous: now is thy mind a fornicator. Thou singest or prayest with thy bodily tongue, but take heed within what thy mind saith. With thy mouth thou blessest, and with thy heart thou cursest. In thy body thou art closed within a strait cell, and in thy cogitation thou wanderest throughout all the world. Thou hearest the word of God with thy corporal ears, rather hear it within. What saith the prophet? Except ye hear within, your soul shall mourn and weep. Yea, and what readest thou in the gospel? that when they see they should not see, and when they hear they should not hear. And again the prophet saith, with your ear ye shall hear and ye shall not perceive. Blessed be they therefore which hear the word of God within. Happy are they to whom God speaketh within, and their souls shall be saved. This ear to incline is commanded, that noble daughter of the king, whose beauty and goodliness is altogether within in golden hems. Finally what availeth it if thou do not those evil things outward, which with affection thou desirest and covetest inward? What availeth it to do good deeds outward, unto which within are committed things clean contrary? Is it so great a thing if thou go to Hierusalem in thy body, when within thine own self is both Sodome, Egypt, and Babylon? is no great thing to have trodden the steps of Christ with thy bodily heels, but it is a great thing to follow the steps of Christ in affection. If it be a very great thing to have touched the sepulchre of Christ, shall it not be also a very great thing to have expressed the mystery of his burying? accusest and utterest thy sins to a priest, which is a man: take heed how thou accusest and utterest them before God, for to accuse them afore him is to hate them inwardly. Thou believest perchance all thy sins and offences to be washed away at once with a little paper or parchment sealed with wax, with a little money or images of wax offered, with a little pilgrimage going. Thou art utterly deceived and clean out of the way. The wound is received inwardly, the medicine therefore must needs be laid to within: thine affection is corrupt, thou hast loved that which was worthy of hate, and hated that which ought to have been beloved. Sweet was to thee sour, and bitter was sweet. I regard not what thou show outward: but and if clean contrary thou shalt begin to hate, to fly, to abhor that which thou lately lovedst, if that wax sweet to thine appetite which lately had the taste of gall: of this wise at the last I perceive and take a token of health. Magdalayne loved much, and many sins were forgiven her. The more thou lovest Christ, the more thou shalt hate vices: for the hate of sin followeth the love of piety as the shadow followeth the body. I had liefer have thee hate once thy vicious manners within and in deed, than to defy them before a priest ten times in word. (as I have rehearsed certain things for love of example) in the whole spectacle and sight of this visible world, in the old law, in the new law, in all the commandments of the church, finally in thyself and in all business appertaining to man, withoutforth is there a certain flesh, and within a spirit. which things if we shall not make a preposterous order, neither in things which are seen shall put very great confidence, but even as they do help to better things, and shall always have respect to the spirit and to things of charity: then shall we wax not heavy as men in sorrow and pain (as those men be) not feeble, ever children (as it is a proverb) not beastly and dry bones (as saith the prophet) without life, drowsy and forgetful as men diseased of the lethargy, not dull having no quickness, not brawlers and scolders, not envious and whisperers or backbiters, but excellent in Christ, in charity, strong and stable both in prosperity and adversity, looking beside small things and enforcing up to things of most profit, full of mirth, full also of knowledge: which knowledge whosoever refuseth them doth that noble lord of all knowledge refuse. For verily ignorance or lack of experience, whom for the most part accompanieth dulness of learning, and that gentlewoman whom the Greeks call Philancia, that is to say, love of thyself, only bringeth to pass (as Esayas saith) that we put confidence in things of nothing, and speak vanities, that we conceive labour and bring forth iniquity, and that we always be fearful and vile bond servants unto the ceremonies of the Jews. Of which manner persons Paul speaking saith, I bear them record that the zeal of God they have, but not after knowledge. But what knew they not? that the end of the law is Christ, and Christ verily is a spirit, he is also charity. But Esayas more plainly describeth the miserable and unprofitable bondage of these men in the flesh: Therefore, saith he, my people be led in captivity because they had no knowledge, and the nobles of them perished for hunger, and the multitude of them dried away for thirst. It is no marvel that the common people be servants to the law and principles of this world, as they which are unlearned, neither have wisdom more than they borrow of other men's heads: it is more to be marvelled that they which are as chief of Christ's religion, in the same captivity perish for hunger, and wither away for thirst. Why perish they for hunger? Because they have not learned of Christ to break barley loaves, they only lick round about the rough and sharp cod or husk, they suck out no marrow or sweet liquor. And why wither they so away for thirst? For because they have not learned of Moses to fetch water out of the spiritual rock of stone, neither have drunk of the rivers of the water of life which floweth, issueth, or springeth out of the belly of Christ: and that was spoken verily of the spirit, not of the flesh. Thou therefore my brother, lest with sorrowful labours thou shouldest not much prevail, but that with mean exercise mightest shortly wax big in Christ and lusty, diligently embrace this rule, and creep not alway on the ground with the unclean beasts, but always sustained with those wings which Plato believeth to spring ever afresh, through the heat of love in the mind of men. up thyself as it were with certain steps of the ladder of Jacob, from the body to the spirit, from the visible world unto the invisible, from the letter to the mystery, from things sensible to things intelligible, from things gross and compound unto things single and pure. Whosoever after this manner shall approach and draw near to the Lord, the Lord of his part shall again approach and draw nigh to him. if thou for thy part shalt endeavour to arise out of the darkness and troubles of the sensual powers, he will come against thee pleasantly and for thy profit, out of his light inaccessible, and out of that noble silence incogitable: in which not only all rage of sensual powers, but also similitudes or imaginations of all the intelligible powers doth cease and keep silence.

The sixth rule

CHAPTER XIV

AND forasmuch as in sudden writing, one thing calleth another to remembrance, I will now add the sixth rule, which is in a manner of kindred to them that go before: a rule for all men as necessary unto health as it is of few regarded. rule is thus, that the mind of him which enforceth and laboureth to Christward, vary as much as is possible both from the deeds and also opinions of the common lay people, and that the example of piety be not set of any other save of Christ only: he is the only chief patron, the only and chief example or form of living, from whom whosoever wrieth one inch or nail breadth, goeth besides the right path and roameth out of the way. Wherefore Plato with gravity, verily as he doth many things in his books of the governance of a city or commonwealth, denieth any man to be able to defend virtue constantly which hath not instructed his mind with sure and undoubted opinions of filthiness and of honesty. But how much more perilous is it if false opinions of the things which pertain to health should sink into the deep bottom of the mind. For that consideration therefore he thinketh that this thing should be cared for and looked upon chiefly, that the governors themselves whom it behoveth to lack all manner of uncleanliness, grave in their own minds very good opinions of things to be ensued and eschewed, that is to say of good and evil, of vices and of virtues, and that they have them very assured, all doubt laid apart as certain laws very holy and goodly: for whatsoever thing cleaveth in the mind surely rooted with steadfast belief, that, every man declareth in his manners and conversation. the chief care of christian men ought to be applied to this point, that their children straightway from the cradle, amongst the very flatterings of the nurses, whiles the father and mother kiss them, may receive and suck under the hands of them which are learned opinions and persuasions meet and worthy of Christ: because that nothing either sinketh deeper or cleaveth faster in the mind than that which (as Fabyus saith) in the young and tender years is poured in. Let be afar off from the ears of little bodies wanton songs of love, which christian men sing at home and wheresoever they ride or go, much more filthy than ever the common people of the heathen men would suffer to be had in use. Let them not hear their mother wail and wring her hands for a little loss of worldly goods, nor for the loss of her sister let them hear her cry out, alas that ever she was born, saying that she is but a wretch, a woman lost or cast away, left alone, desolate and destitute. Let them not hear their father rebuking and upbraiding him of cowardice which hath not recompensed injury or wrong with double: neither yet lauding them which have gathered together great abundance of worldly substance, by whatsoever manner it were. The disposition of man is frail and prone to vices, he catcheth mischievous example at once: none otherwise than tow catcheth fire if it be put to. How be it this selfsame thing is to be done in every age, that all the errors of the lay people might be plucked out again from the mind by the hard roots, and in their places might be planted wholesome opinions, and so might be roborate that with no violence they could be shaken or plucked asunder: which thing whosoever hath done shall easily and without business by his own accord follow virtue, and shall account them that do otherwise worthy to be lamented and pitied, and not to be counterfeited or followed. this thing pertaineth that not indiscreet saying of Socrates (though it were rebuked of Aristotle), that virtue was nothing else but the knowledge of things to be ensued and followed, and of things to be eschewed or fled: not but that Socrates saw the difference between knowledge of honesty and the love of the same. But as Demosthenes answered, pronunciation to be the first, the second, and also the third point of eloquence, signifying that to be the chief part, in so much that he thought eloquence to rest altogether in that thing only: in likewise Socrates, disputing with Prothagoras, proveth by arguments, knowledge in all virtue to bear such room, that vices can no other whence proceed than of false opinions. certainly, brother, both he that loveth Christ, and he also that loveth voluptuousness, money, false honour, doth follow that thing which is to either of them sweet, good, and beautiful, but the one slideth through ignorance, instead of a sweet thing embracing a thing out of measure sour, fleeing as a sour thing that which is sweetest of all: also following that thing for good and for lucre which is naught else but damage and loss, and fearing that thing for loss, which is chief gains or advantage: and judging that thing to be fair which is foul, and weening or trowing that to be shameful which only is glorious and praiseful. In conclusion, if a man were surely and inwardly brought in belief, and if also it were digested in to the substance of his mind as meat in to the substance of the body, that only virtue were best, most sweet, most fair, most honest, most profitable. And on the other side filthiness only to be an evil thing, a painful torment or punishment, a foul thing, shameful, full of damage or loss: and did measure these things not by the opinion of the common people, but by the very nature of the things, it could not be (such persuasion or belief enduring) that he should stick fast and cleave long time in evil things. For now long ago the common people is found to be the most mischievous author or captain both of living and also of judgment: was the world ever in so good state and condition, but that the worst hath pleased the most part. Beware lest thou this wise think: no man is there that doth not this, mine elders before me have walked in these steps, of this opinion is such a man, so great a philosopher, so great a divine: this is the custom and manner of living of kings, this wise live great men, this do both bishops and popes, these verily are no common people. Let not these great names move thee one inch. I measure or judge not the common or rascal sort by the room, estate, or degree, but by the mind and stomach. Whosoever in the famous cave of Plato bound with the bonds of their own affections wonder at the vain images and shadows of things instead of very true things, they be the common people. he not do preposterously or out of order if a man would go about to try not the stone by the ruler or square, but the ruler by the stone? And were it not much more unreasonable if a man would go about to bow and turn, not the manners of men to Christ, but Christ to the living of men? Think it not therefore well or aright because that great men or because that the most men do it, but this wise only shall it be well and right whatsoever is done, if it agree to the rule of Christ: yea and therefore ought a thing to be suspected because it pleaseth the most part. It is a small flock and ever shall be, to whom is pleasant the simplicity or plainness, the poverty, the verity of Christ. It is a small flock verily but a blessed, as unto whom doubtless is due only the kingdom of heaven. Strait is the way of virtue and of very few trodden on, but none other leadeth to life. To conclude, whether doth a wise builder fetch his example of the most common and used or of the best work? Painters set afore them none but the best tables or patrons of imagery. Our example is Christ, in whom only be all rules of blessed living, him may we counterfeit without exception. But in good and virtuous men it shall be meet that thou call to example everything, so far forth as it shall agree with the first example of Christ. touching the common sort of christian men think thus, that they were never more corrupt, no not amongst the gentiles, as appertaining to the opinions of their manners. as touching their faith what opinions they have advise them. This surely is doubtless and to be abidden by, faith without manners worthy of faith prevaileth nothing, insomuch also that it groweth to a heap of damnation. the histories of antiquity, to them compare the manners that be now-a-days. When was virtue and true honesty more despised? When was so had in price riches gotten not regarded whence? In what world at any time was truer that saying of Horacius: that lady money giveth a wife with dowry, credence, friendship, nobleness, noble kin and also beauty. And again this saying of the same Horace, nobleness and virtue, except a man have good withal, is viler than a rush or a straw. Who readeth not in good earnest that biting mock of the same poet: Oh citizens, citizens, first seek money, after seek virtue. When was riot or excess more immoderate than now? When was adultery and all other kinds of unchaste living either more appert in the sight of every man, or more unpunished, or else less had in shame, rebuke or abomination? While princes favour their own vices, in other men suffering them unpunished, and every man accounteth that most comely and beautiful to be done whatsoever is used and taken up among courtiers. To whom seemeth not poverty extreme evil, and uttermost shame and rebuke? time past against keepers of queans, filthy nigards, glorious or gorgeous persons, lovers and regarders of money, were cast in the teeth with rebukeful and slanderous scoffings and jestings, yea with authority. And also in comedies, tragedies, and other common plays of the gentiles a great clapping of hands and a shout was made for joy of the lay people, when vices were craftily and properly rebuked and checked: at the which same vices now-a-days being evil praised there is made a shout and clapping of hands for joy even of the nobles and estates of christian men. The Athenes in their common house appointed for disguisings and interludes could not forbear nor suffer a jester in playing a certain tragedy of Euripides, to sing the words of a certain covetous man which preferred money only before all other commodities and pleasure of man's life: they would plainly have clapped out of the play, yea and violently cast out of the house the player with all the fable, except the poet by and by arising up had desired them to tarry a little and behold to what point that so great a wonderer at money should come. How many examples be there in the histories of gentiles, of them which of the commonwealth well governed and ministered brought nothing in to their poor household but an honest opinion or reputation: which set more by fidelity than money, by chastity than by life, whom neither prosperity could make proud, wild and wanton, neither adversity could overcome and make heavy hearted, which regarded honest jeopardies and dangers before voluptuousness and pleasures, which contented only with the conscience of pure life, desired neither honours, neither riches, nor any other commodities of fortune. And to overhyp and make no rehearsal of the holiness of Phocion, of poverty of Fabricius more excellent than riches, of the strong and courageous mind of Camyllus, of the strait and indifferent justice of

Brutus, of the chastity of Pithagoras, of the temperance of Socrates, of the sound and constant virtue of Cato: a thousand most goodly beams of all sorts of virtues which are read everywhere in the histories of the Lacedemones, of the Perces, of the Athenes, and of the Romanes, to our great shame verily. Holy Aurelius Augustyne, as he of himself witnesseth in the commentaries of his own confessions, long time before he put Christ on him despised money, counted honours for naught, was not moved with glory, praise, or fame, and to voluptuousness kept the bridle so strait that he then a young man was content with one little wench, to whom he kept also promise and faith of marriage. examples among courtiers, among men of the church: I will also say amongst religious persons, shall not a man lightly find; or else if any such shall be, by and by he shall be pointed, wondered, or mocked at as it were an ass among apes: he shall be called with one voice of all men a doting fool, a gross head, an hypocrite in nothing expert, melancholy mad, and shall not be judged to be a man. So we christian men honour the doctrine of Christ: so counterfeit we it that every where now-a-days nothing is accounted more foolish, more vile, more to be ashamed of, than to be a christian man indeed, with all the mind and heart: as though that either Christ in vain had been conversant in earth, or that christendom were some other thing now than in time past, or as it indifferently pertained not to all men. will therefore that thou from these men vary with all thy mind, and esteem the value of everything by the communion or fellowship of Christ only. thinketh it not everywhere to be an excellent thing, and to be numbered among the chief of all good things, if a man descend of a worshipful stock and of honourable ancestors, which thing they call nobleness? it not move thee one whit when thou hearest the wise men of this world, men of sadness endued with great authority, so earnestly disputing of the degrees of their genealogies or lineage, having their forehead and upper brows drawn together with very great gravity, as it were a matter of marvellous difficulty, yea and with great enforcement bringing forth plain trifles. Nor let it move thee when thou seest other so high minded for the noble acts of their grandfathers or great grandfathers, that think other in comparison of themselves scarce to be men: but thou laughing at the error of these men after the manner of Democrytus shalt count (as true it is indeed) that the only and most perfect nobleness is to be regenerate in Christ, to be grafted and planted in the body of him, to be one body and one spirit with God. Let other men be kings' sons: to thee let it be greatest honour that can be, that thou art called, and art so indeed, the son of God. them stand in their own conceits, because they are daily conversant in great princes' courts: choose thou rather to be with David, vile abject in the house of God. Take heed what manner fellows Christ chooseth, feeble persons, fools, vile as touching this world. In Adam we are all born of low degree. In Christ we are all one thing, neither high nor low of degree one more than another. Very nobleness is to despise this vain nobleness: very nobleness is to be servant to Christ. Think them to be thine ancestors whose virtues thou both lovest and counterfeitest. Also hark what the true esteemer of nobleness said in the gospel against the Jews which boasted themselves to be of the generation of Abraham: a man verily not excellent only, not rich only, not the conqueror of kings only, but also for his divine virtues lauded of God himself. Who would not think this to be a noble thing and worthy whereof a man might rejoice? Hark yet what they heard: ye are (said Christ) of your father the devil, and the deeds of your father ye do. hear also Paul, how he esteemeth gentle blood, according to his master's rule: Not all they (saith he) which be of circumcision of Israel be Israelites, neither all they that be of the seed of Abraham be the sons of Abraham. It is a low degree and shameful to serve filthiness, and to have no kindred with Christ which acknowledgeth kindred with no man but with such as fulfilleth the will of his Father in heaven. He is with much shame a bastard which hath the devil to his father, and verily whosoever doth the deeds of the devil hath the devil to his father, except Christ lied: but the truth cannot lie. The highest degree that can be is to be the son and heir ot God, the brother and co-heir with Christ: what their badges and cognisances mean let them take heed. badges of Christ be common to all men, and the most honourable, which be the cross, the crown of thorn, the nails, the spear, the signs or tokens which Paul rejoiceth to bear in his body. Of nobleness therefore thou seest how much otherwise I would have thee to judge and think than the lay people imagine. Who calleth not him blessed, rich, and happy among the common people which hath heaped together at home a great deal of gold? judge thou him to be blessed enough, yea that he only is blessed which possesseth Christ, very felicity, and of all things the best. Judge him happy which hath bought the noble and precious margaryte of pure mind with the loss either of all his goods or his body also, which hath found the treasure of wisdom preciouser than all riches, which to be made rich hath bought of Christ, that is most rich, gold purified and proved with fire. What things then be these which the common people wondereth at, as gold, precious stones, livelihood? a wrong name they be riches, in the true name they be very thorns, which choke the seed of the word of God, according to the parable of the Gospel. They be packs or fardels with which whosoever be laden neither can follow poor Christ by strait way, neither enter by the low door into the kingdom of heaven. not thyself better by one hair if thou shouldest pass in riches either Mydas or Cresus, but think thyself more bound, more tangled, more laden. He hath abundantly enough that can utterly despise such things. He is provided for sufficiently to whom Christ promised nothing should be lacking. He shall not be an hungered to whose mouth manna of the word of God seemeth pleasant. He shall not be naked which hath put Christ upon him. this only to be a loss, as oft as any thing of godliness is minished, and anything of vices is increased. Think it a great lucre or advantage when thy mind through increase of virtue is waxed better. Think thou lackest nothing as long as thou possessest him in whom is all things. But what is this which wretches call pleasure? Surely it is nothing less than that it is called. What is it then? Pure madness it is, and plainly (as Greeks be wont to say) the laughter of Ayax, sweet poison, pleasant mischief. and only pleasure is the inward joy of a pure conscience. The most noble and daintiest dish that can be is the study of holy scripture. The most delectable songs be the psalms indited of the Holy Ghost. The most pleasant fellowship is the communion of all saints. The highest dainties of all is the fruition and enjoying of the very truth. Purge now thy eyes, purge thy ears, purge thy mouth, and Christ shall begin to wax sweet and pleasant to thee which tasted once sourly: yea, if Milesii Sibarite, if all incontinent rioters and epicureans, shortly if the university of imaginers and devisers of pleasures should heap together all their flattering subtleties and dainty dishes, in comparison of him only they shall seem to provoke ye to spue. That is not by and by sweet which is savoury, but that which is savoury to a whole man: if water have the taste of wine to him which burneth in a hot fever, no man will call that a pleasure but a disease. Thou art deceived if thou believe not that the very tears be much more pleasant to devout and holy men than be to wicked men laughings, mockings, jestings or scoffings: if thou also believe not fasting to be sweeter to the one than to the other plovers, quails, pheasants, partridges, pike, trout, porpoise, or the fresh sturgeon. And the moderate boards of the one appointed with herbs and fruits to be much more delicate than the costly and disdainful feasts of the other. Finally the true pleasure is, for the love of Christ not to be once moved with false apparent pleasures. Behold now how much the world abuseth the names of love and hate. a foolish young man is clear out of his wit and mad for a wench's sake, that the common people calleth love, and yet is there no verier hate in the world. True love even with his own loss desireth to see unto another man's profit. Whereunto looketh he save unto his own pleasure, therefore he loveth not her but himself: yet loveth he not himself verily, for no man can love another except he love himself first, yea and except he love himself aright. No man can hate any man at all except he first hate himself. Nevertheless sometime to love well is to hate well, and to hate well is to love well. Whosoever therefore for his little pleasure (as he supposeth it) layeth await and goeth about to beguile a maiden with flattering and gifts, with fair promises to pluck from her the best thing she hath, that is to wit her perfectness, her chastity, her simplicity, her innocency, her good mind, and her good name, whether seemeth this man to hate or to love? Certainly there is no hate more cruel than is this hate, when the foolish father and mother favour the vices of their children: the common saying is, how tenderly love they their children. I pray thee how cruelly hate they their children which (while they follow their own affections) regard not at all the wealth of their children. What other wisheth to us our most hateful enemy the devil, than that we here sinning unpunished should fall into eternal punishment? They call him an easy master and a merciful prince, which at certain grievous offences either wink or favour them, that the more unpunished men sin, the more boldly and at large they might sin. But what other thing threateneth God by his prophet to them whom he judgeth unworthy of his mercy? I will not (saith he) visit their daughters when they commit fornication, nor their daughters-in-law when they commit adultery. Unto David what promised he? I will (saith he) with a rod look upon their iniquities, and with whips their sins, but I will not take my mercy from them. Thou seest how all things are renewed in Christ, and how the names of things are changed. Whosoever love himself otherwise than well, hateth himself deadly. Whosoever be evil merciful toward himself is a tyrant most cruel. To care well is not to regard. To hurt well is to do good. To destroy well is to save. Thou shalt care well for thyself if thou shalt despise the desires of the flesh, if in good manner thou shalt rage against vices, thou shalt do to the man a good turn. If thou shalt kill the sinner thou shalt save the man. If thou shalt destroy that man hath made, thou shalt restore that God hath made. Come off now and let us go further: What thinketh the error of the people, power, wickedness, manhood, and cowardness to be? Call they not him mighty which can lightly hurt whom him list? though it be a very odious power to be able to hurt, for in that are they resembled to noisome worms and scorpions, and to the devil himself, that is to wit in doing harm. Only God is mighty indeed, which neither can hurt if he would, neither yet would if he could, for his nature is to do good. But this mighty fellow, how doth he I beseech thee hurt a man? He shall take away thy money? He shall beat thy body? He shall rob thee of thy life? If he do it to him that feareth God well, he hath done a good deed instead of an evil: but and if he have done it to an evil man, the one hath ministered an occasion verily, but the other hath hurt himself: for no man is hurt but of himself. No man goeth about to hurt another except the same man hath much more grievously hurt himself aforehand. Thou enforcest to hurt me in my money or goods. Now hast thou through the loss of charity hurt thyself most grievously. Thou canst not fasten a wound in me, but if thou have received a wound much more grievous. Thou canst not take from me the life of my body, unless thou have slain thine own soul before. But Paul, which to do wrong was a man very weak and feeble, to suffer wrong most valiant and strong, rejoiceth that he could do all thing in Christ. They call him everywhere manly and bold which being fierce and of impotent mind, for the least displeasure that can be rageth, seetheth, or boileth in wrath, and acquitteth a shrewd word with a shrewd word, a check with a check, one evil turn with another. On the other side whosoever when he hath received wrong maketh nothing ado, but dissimuleth as no such thing were done, him they call a coward, a bastard, heartless, meet for nothing: yea but what is more contrary to the greatness of the mind than with a little word to be put aside from the quiet and constancy of the spirit, and to be so unable to set at naught another man's foolishness, that thou shouldest think thyself to be no man except thou shouldest overcome one shrewd turn with another. But how much more manful is it with an excellent and large mind to be able to despise all manner injuries, and moreover for an evil deed to recompense a good? would not call him a bold man which durst jeopard on his enemy, which scale castle or town walls, which (his life not regarded) putteth himself in all manner jeopardies, a thing common almost to all warriors, but whosoever could overcome his own mind, whosoever could will them good which doth him harm, pray for them which curse him. To this man is due the proper name of a bold and strong man and of excellent mind. Let us also discuss another thing, what the world calleth praise, rebuke, and shame. art praised, for what cause and of whom? If for filthy things and of filthy persons, this verily is a false praise and a true rebuke. Thou art dispraised, thou art mocked or laughed at, for what cause and of whom? For godliness and innocency, and that of evil men: this is not a rebuke, no, there is no truer praise. Be it that all the world reprove, refuse, and disallow it, yet can it not be but glorious and of great praise that Christ approveth. And though whatsoever is in the world agree, consent, and allow, crying with a shout that is a noble deed, yet can it not be but shameful that displeaseth God. call wisdom everywhere, to get good stoutly, when it is gotten to maintain it lustily, and to provide long before for the time to come: for so we hear them say everywhere and in good earnest of them which in short time get substance somewhat abundantly, he is a thrifty man, ware and wise, circumspect and provident. Thus saith the world which is both a liar himself and also his father. But what saith verity: Fool, saith he, I will set again this night thy soul from thee. He had filled his barns with corn, he had stuffed his storehouses with provision of all victuals, and had laid up at home abundantly of money enough: he thought nothing was to be done more. Thus had he done, not because he intended as a needy keeper to sit abroad on his riches heaped together, as the poets feign the dragon to have kept the golden fleece (which thing men do almost everywhere), but he intended to have spent joyously, and yet doth the gospel call this man a fool. For what is more foolish, what is more gross imagination or more fondness than to gape at the shadows, lose the very things, a thing which we be wont to laugh at in the famous dog of Ysope: and in the manners of christian men is it not more to be laughed at, or rather to be wept at? He may be counted a rude and unexpert merchant that knew not this saying of Terence: To refuse money at a season is sometime a great advantage, or whosoever would receive a little advantage in hand when he knew great loss should follow. How much more foolishness and unadvisedness is it to make provision with so great care for this present life which is but a shadow, every hour ready to fail: namely when God (if we believe the gospel) will minister all thing necessary for this life, if we have confidence in him, and for the life to come to make no provision at all, which we must lead alway full of misery and wretchedness, if provision be not made now aforehand with great diligence. Hear another error: they call him peerless, politic and in all things expert, which hearkening for all manner tidings knoweth what is done throughout all the world, what is the chance of merchandise, what the king of England intendeth, new thing is done at Rome, what is chanced in France, how the Danes and the Sytes live, what matters great princes have in council: to make an end shortly, whoever can babble with all kinds of men of all manner business, him they say to be wise. But what can be farther from the thought of a wise man, or near to the nature of a fool, than to search for those things which be done afar off and pertain to thee nothing at all, and not so much as once verily to think on those things which are done in thine own breast and pertain to thee only. Thou tellest me of the trouble and business of England, tell me rather what trouble maketh in thy breast, wrath, envy, bodily lust, ambition, how nigh these be brought into subjection, what hope is of victory, how much of this host is put to flight, how reason is decked or appointed. In these things if thou shalt be watching and have a quick ear and also an eye, if thou shalt smell, if thou shalt be circumspect, I will call thee politic and peerless: and that thing which the world is wont to cast against us, I will hurl again at him: he is not wise at all, which is not wise for his own profit. After this manner if thou shalt examine all the cares of mortal men, their joys, hopes, fears, studies, their minds or judgments, thou shalt find all thing full of error while they call good evil, and evil good, while they make sweet sour and sour sweet, make light darkness and darkness light. And this sort of men is the most part by a great deal. Notwithstanding thou must even at once both defy them and set no store of them, lest thou shouldest be minded to be like them: and also pity them so that thou wouldest fain have them like unto thee. And to use the words of Saint Augustyn: then is it meet both to weep for them which are worthy to be laughed at, and to laugh at them which are worthy to be wept for. Be not in evil things conformable to this world but be reformed in the new wit, that thou mayst approve not those things which men wonder at, but what is the will of God, which is good, well pleasing and perfect. Thou art very nigh jeopardy and no doubt fallest suddenly from the true way if thou shalt begin to look about thee what the most part of men do, and to hearken what they think or imagine: but suffer thou, which art the child of life and of light also, that dead men bury their dead bodies: and let the blind captains of blind men go away together into the ditch: see thou once move not the eyes of thy heart any whither from the first patron and chief example of Christ. shalt not go out of the way, if thou follow the guiding of verity. Thou shalt not stumble in darkness, if thou walk after light, the light shining before thee: if thou shalt separate coloured good things, from good things indeed: and evil things indeed from apparent evil things: thou shalt abhor and not counterfeit the blindness of the common people, and chafing themselves after the manner of the ebbing and flowing of the sea at the most vain illusions and worldly things, with certain caresses of affections of wrath, envy, love, hate, hope, fear, joy, sorrow, raging more un-quietly than any Euripus. The Bragmanyes, Cynikes, Stoikes be wont to defend their principles stiffly with tooth and nail: and even the whole world repugning, all men crying and darkening against them, yet hold they stiffly that thing whereunto they once have given sure credence. thou bold likewise to fasten surely in thy mind the decrees of thy sect. Be bold without mistrust, and with all that thou canst, make to follow the mind of thine author, departing from all contrary opinions and sects.

Here follow opinions meet for a Christian man

CHAPTER XV

LET this excellent learning and paradoxes of the true christian faith be sure and stedfast with thee, that no christian man may think that he is born for himself: neither ought to have the mind to live to himself: but whatsoever he hath, whatsoever he is, that altogether let him ascribe not to himself, unto God the author thereof, and of whom it came, all his goods let him think to be common to all men. The charity of a christian man knoweth no property: let him love good men in Christ, evil men for Christ's sake, which so loved us first when we were yet his enemies, that he bestowed himself on us altogether for our redemption: let him embrace the one because they be good: the other nevertheless to make them good: he shall hate no man at all, no more verily than a faithful physician hateth a sick man: let him be an enemy only unto vices: the greater the disease is, the greater cure will pure charity put thereto: he is an adulterer, he hath committed sacrilege, he is a Turk: a christian man defy the adulterer, not the man: let him despise the committer of sacrilege, not the man: let him kill the Turk, not the man: let him find the means that the evil man perish such as he hath made himself to be, but let the man be saved whom God made: let him will well, wish well, and do well, to all men unfeign-edly: neither hurt them which have deserved it, but do good to them which have not deserved it; let him be glad of all men's commodities as well as of his own, and also be sorry for all men's harms none otherwise than for his own. For verily this is that which the apostle commandeth: to weep with them that weep, to joy with them that joy, yea let him rather take another man's harm grievouser than his own: and of his brother's wealth be gladder than of his own. It is not a christian man's part to think on this wise: what have I to do with this fellow, I know not whether he be black or white, he is unknown to me, he is a stranger to me, he never did aught for me, he hath hurt me some-time, but did me never good. Think none of these things: remember only for what deserving can those things which Christ hath done for thee, which would his kindness done to thee, should be recompensed, not in himself, but in thy neighbour. Only see of what things he hath need, and what thou art able to do for him. Think this thing only, he is my brother in our Lord, co-heir in Christ, a member of the same body, redeemed with one blood, a fellow in the common faith, called unto the very same grace and felicity of the life to come, even as the apostle said, one body and one spirit as ye be called in one hope of your calling, one lord and one faith, one baptism, one God, and father of all which is above all and everywhere, and in all us. How can he be a stranger to whom thou art coupled with so manifold bonds of unity? Among the gentiles let those circumstances of rhetoricians be of no little value and weight, either unto benevolence or unto malevolence, he is a citizen of the same city, he is of alliance, he is my cousin, he is my familiar friend, he is my father's friend, he hath well deserved, he is kind, born of an honest stock, rich or otherwise. In Christ all these things either be nothing, or after the mind of Paul be all one, and the very selfsame thing: let this be ever present before thine eyes and let this suffice thee, he is my flesh, he is my brother in Christ. Whatsoever is bestowed upon any member reboundeth it not to all the body, and from thence into the head? We all be members each one of another, members cleaving together make a body. The head of the body is Jesu Christ, the head of Christ is God. It is done to thee it is done to everyone, it is done to Christ it is done to God: whatsoever is done to any one member whichsoever it be, whether it be well done or evil: All these things are one, God, Christ, the body, and the members. That saying hath no place conveniently among christian men, like with like. And the other saying, diversity is mother of hate: for unto what purpose pertain words of dissension where so great unity is, it savoureth not of christian faith that commonly a courtier to a town dweller: one of the country to an inhabiter of the city: a man of high degree, to another of low degree: an officer, to him that is officeless: the rich to the poor: a man of honour, to a vile person: the mighty to the weak: the Italyen to the Germayne: the Frenssheman to the Englysshman: the Englysshe to the Scotte: the grammarian to the divine: the logician to the grammarian: the physician to the man of law: the learned to the unlearned: the eloquent to him that is not facounde and lacketh utterance: the single to the married: the young to the old; the clerk to the layman: the priest to the monk: the Carmelytes to the Jacobytes: and that (lest I rehearse all diversities) in a very trifle unlike to unlike, is somewhat partial and unkind: where is charity which loveth even his enemy: the surname changed, when the colour of the vesture a little altered, when the girdle or the shoe and like fantasies of men make me hated unto thee? Why rather leave we not these childish trifles, and accustom to have before our eyes that which pertaineth to the very thing: whereof Paul warneth us in many places, that all we in Christ our head be members of one body, endued with life by one spirit (if so be we live in him) so that we should neither envy the happier members, and should gladly succour and aid the weak members: that we might perceive that we ourselves have received a good turn, when we have done any benefit to our neighbour: and that we ourselves be hurt, when hurt is done to our brother: and that we might understand how no man ought to study privately for himself, every man for his own part should bestow in common that thing which he hath received of God, that all things might redound and rebound thither again, from whence they sprung, that is to wit, from the head. This verily is the thing which Paul writeth to the Corynthes, saying, As the body is one and hath many members, and all the members of the body though they be many, yet be they but one body: even so likewise is Christ, for in one spirit we be all baptised to make one body, whether we be Jews or gentiles, whether we be bond or free, and all we have drunk of one spirit, for the body (saith Paul) is not one member but many: if the foot shall say, I am not the hand, I am not of the body: is he therefore not of the body? If the ear shall say, I am not the eye, I am not of the body: is he therefore not of the body? If all the body should be the eye, where is then the hearing: if all the body were the hearing, where then should be the smelling? But now God hath put the members every one of them in the body, as it pleased him: for if all were but one member, where were the body? but now verily be there many members, yet but one body. The eye cannot say to the hand I have no need of thy help, or again the head to the feet, ye be not to me necessary: but those members of the body which seem to be the weaker are much more necessary: and to those which we think to be the viler members of the body we give more abundant honour: and those which be our unhonest members have more abundant honesty, for our honest members have need of nothing. But God hath tempered and ordered the body, giving plenteous honour to that part which lacked, because there should be no division, debate or strife in the body, but that the members should care one for another indifferently. But it is ye which are the body of Christ and members one depending of another. He writeth like things to the Romans, saying, in one body we have many members, and all members have not one office. so we being many are but one body in Christ: but singularly we be members each one of another, having gifts divers after the grace which is given to us. And again to the Epheses. Working verity (saith he) in charity, let us in all manner things grow in him which is the head, that is to wit Christ, in whom all the body compact and knit by every joint, whereby one part ministereth to another according to the operation and virtue which springeth of the head and capacity of every member, in receiving maketh the increase of the body for the edifying of himself in charity. And in another place he biddeth every man to bear one another's burden, because we be members one of another. Look then whether they pertain unto this body whom thou hearest speaking everywhere after this manner, it is my good, it came to me by inheritance, I possess it by right and not by fraud, why shall not I use it and abuse it after mine own mind, why should I give them of it any deal at all to whom I owe nothing? I spill, I waste, I destroy, that which perisheth is mine own, it maketh no matter to other men. Thy member complaineth and grinneth for hunger and thou spuest up partridges. Thy naked brother shivereth for cold, and with thee so great plenty of raiment is corrupt with moths and long lying. One night's dicing hath lost thee a thousand pieces of gold, while in the mean season some wretched wench (need compelling her) hath set forth her chastity to sell, and is become a common harlot, and thus perisheth the soul for whom Christ hath bestowed his life. Thou sayest again: what is that to me? I entreat that which is mine own after mine own fashion: and after all this with this so corrupt mind thinkest thou thyself to be a christian man, which art not once a man verily? Thou hearest in the presence of a great multitude the good name or fame of this or that man to be hurt, thou holdest thy peace, or peradventure rejoicest and art well content with the backbiter. Thou sayest, I would have reproved him if those things which were spoken had pertained to me, but I have nothing ado with him which was there slandered. Then to conclude, thou hast nothing ado with the body, if thou have nothing ado with the member, neither hast thou aught ado with the head, verily, if the body nothing appertain to thee. A man (say they now-a-days) with violence may defend and put aback violence: what the Emperour's laws permit I pass not thereon. This I marvel, how these voices came in to the manners of christian men. I hurt him, but I was provoked, I had liefer hurt than be hurt. Be it man's laws punish not that which they have permitted. But what will the Emperour Christ do, if thou beguile his law which is written in Matthew? command you (saith Christ there) not once to withstand harm: but if a man shall give thee a blow on the right cheek, offer to him also the other. And whosoever will strive with thee in the law, and take from thee thy coat, yield up to him also thy cloak or mantle. And whosoever shall compel thee to go with him one mile, go with him two more other. Love your enemies, and do good to them which hate you, and pray for them which persecute you and pick matters against you, that ye may be the sons of your father which is in heaven, which maketh the sun to rise upon good and evil, and sendeth rain upon just and unjust. Thou answerest, he spake not this to me, he spake it to his apostles, he spake it to perfect persons. Heardest thou not how he said that ye may be the sons of your father? if thou care not to be the son of God, that law pertaineth not to thee. ess he is not good verily which would not be perfect. Hark also another thing: if thou desire no reward, the commandment belongeth not to thee: for it followeth. If ye love them which love you, what reward shall ye have? as who should say, none: for verily, to do these things (that is to say, to love them that loveth thee) is not virtue: but not to do it, is an evil thing: there is debt of neither side where is just recompense made of both sides. Hear Paul, both a great wise man and cunning and an interpreter also of Christ's law. Bless (saith he) them that persecute you, bless them, and curse them in no wise, rendering to no man evil for evil, if it may be as much as in you is, having rest and peace with all men, not defending yourself, my best beloved brethren, but give place and withstand ye not wrath: for it is written, Vengeance shall be reserved to me and I will requite them saith our Lord. But if thine enemy shall be hungry, give to him meat: if he be athirst, give to him drink: for if thou do this, thou shalt heap coals of fire upon his head, that is to say, thou shalt make him to love fervently. Be not overcome of evil, but overcome evil in goodness. What shall then follow, sayest thou, if I shall with my softness nourish up the knappyshnes or malice and froward audacity of another man, and in suffering an old injury provoke a new? If thou can without thine own evil either avoid or put by evil, no man forbiddeth thee to do it: but if not, look thou say not, it is better to do than to suffer. thine enemy if thou can, either lading him with benefits, or overcoming him with meekness: if that help not, it is better that the one perish than both: it is better that thou wax rich with the lucre and advantage of patience than that while either to other rendereth evil both be made evil. Let this therefore be a decree among christian men, to compare with all men in love, in meekness, and in benefits, or doing good: in striving, hate or backbiting, in rebukes and injury, to give place ever to them that be of lowest degree, and that with good will. But he is unworthy to whom a good turn should be done, or an evil forgiven, yet is it meet for thee to do it, and Christ is worthy for whose sake it is done. I will neither (say they) hurt any man, neither suffer myself to be hurt: yet when thou art hurt, see thou forgive the trespass with all thy heart, providing always that nothing be which any man should remit or forgive unto thee. Be as ware and diligent in avoiding that none offence or trespass proceed from thee, as thou art easy and ready to remit another man's. greater man thou art, so much the more submit thyself, that thou in charity apply thyself to all men. thou come of a noble stock, manners worthy of Christ shall not dishonour, but honour the nobleness of thy birth. thou be cunning and well learned, so much the more soberly suffer and amend the ignorance of the unlearned. The more is committed and lent to thee, the more art thou bound to thy brother. art rich, remember thou art the dispenser, not the lord: take heed circumspectly how thou entreatest the common good. thou that property or impropriation was prohibit and voluntary poverty enjoined to monks only? Thou art deceived, both pertain indifferently to all christian men. The law punisheth thee if thou take away anything of another man's: it punisheth not if thou withdraw thine own from thy needy brother: but Christ will punish both. If thou be an officer, let not the honour make thee more fierce, but let the charge make thee more diligent and fuller of care. I bear not (sayest thou) no office of the church, I am not a shepherd or a bishop. Let us grant you that, but also art thou not a christian man, consider thou of whence thou art, if thou be not of the church. So greatly Christ is coming into contempt to the world, that they think it a goodly and excellent thing to have nothing to do with him: and that so much the more every man should be despised, the more coupled he were to him. Hearest thou not daily of the lay persons in their fury, the names of a clerk, of a priest, of a monk, to be cast in our teeth, instead of a sharp and cruel rebuke, saying, thou clerk, thou priest, thou monk, that thou art: and it is done, utterly with none other mind, with none other voice or pronouncing, than if they should cast in our teeth incest or sacrilege. verily marvel why they also cast not in our teeth baptism, why also object they not against us with the Sarazyns the name of Christ as an opprobrious thing. If they said, an evil clerk, an unworthy priest, or an unreligious monk, in that they might be suffered as men which note the manners of the persons, and not despise the profession of virtue. But whosoever counteth praise in themselves the deflowering of virgins, good taken away in war, money either won or lost at dice or other chance, and have nothing to lay against another man more spiteful or opprobrious or more to be ashamed of, than the names of a monk or a priest. Certainly it is easy to conjecture what these, in name only christian men, judge of Christ. There is not one Lord of the bishops and another of the temporal officers, but both be under one, and to the same both must give accounts: If thou look any other where save unto him only, either when thou receivest the office or when thou ministerest it, it maketh no matter though the world call thee not a symonyake, he surely will punish thee as a symonyake. thou labour and make means to obtain a common office, not to profit in common, but to provide for thine own wealth privately, and to avenge thyself of them to whom thou owest a grudge, thy office is bribery or robbery afore God. Thou huntest after thieves not that he should receive his own that is robbed, but lest it should not be with thee which is with the thieves. How much difference I pray thee is there between the thieves and thee, except peradventure that they be the robbers of merchants, and thou the robber of robbers. conclusion, except thou bear thine office with this mind, that thou be ready, and that with the loss, I will not say of thy goods but, of thy life to defend that which is right, Christ will not approve thy administration. I will add also another thing of the mind or judgment of Plato: no man is worthy of an office which is gladly in an office. thou be a prince, beware lest these perilous witches, the voices of flatterers, do enchant or bewitch thee. Thou art a lord, over the laws thou art free, whatsoever thou doest is honest, to thee is lawful whatsoever thou list. Those things pertain not to thee which are preached daily of priests to the common people: yea, but think thou rather which is true, that there is one master over all men, he is Christ Jesus, to whom thou oughtest to be as like as is possible, to whom thou oughtest to conform thyself in all things, as unto him certainly whose authority or room thou bearest. No man ought to follow his doctrine more straitly than thou, of whom he will ask accounts more straitly than of other. Think not straightway that to be right that thou wilt, but only will thou which is right. Whatsoever may be filthy to any man in the world, see that thou think not that an honest thing to thee, but see thou in no wise permit to thyself any thing which is used to be forgiven and pardoned among the common sort. which in other men is but a small trespass, think in thyself to be a great outrage or excess. Let not thy riches greater than the common people bring unto thee honour, reverence, and dignity, favour, and authority: but let thy manners better than the common people's utterly deserve them. not the common people to wonder at those things in thee, wherewith are provoked and enticed the very same mischievous deeds which thou punishest daily. Take away this wondering and praise of riches, and where be thieves, where be oppressors of the commonwealth, where be committers of sacrilege, where be errant thieves and robbers or rievers: take away wondering at voluptuousness, and where be ravishers of women, where be adulterers? As often as thou wilt appear somewhat according after thy degree among thy friends and subjects or them over whom thou bearest office, room or authority, set not open thy riches and treasure to the eyes of foolish persons. When thou wilt seem somewhat wealthy, shew not in boast the riotous example of expense and voluptuousness. First of all let them learn in thee to despise such things, let them learn to honour virtue, to have measure in price, to rejoice in temperance, to give honour to sober lowliness or meekness. Let none of those things be seen in thy manners and conversation, which thine authority punisheth in the manners and conversation of the people. Thou shalt banish evil deeds in the best wise, if men shall not see riches and voluptuous-

ness, the matter and ground of evil deeds to be magnified in thee. Thou shalt
not despise in comparison of thyself any man, no not the vilest of the lowest
degree, for common and indifferent is the price wherewith ye both were redeemed. Let not the noise of ambition, neither fierceness, neither weapons, nor
men of the guard, defend thee from contempt, but pureness of living, gravity,
manners uncorrupt and sound from all manner vices of the common people.
forbiddeth (in bearing rule) to keep the chief room, and yet in charity to
discern no room. Think bearing of room or rule to be this, not to excel and go
before other men in abundance of riches, but to profit all men as much as is
possible. Turn not to thine own profit things which are common, but bestow
those things which be thine own, and thine own self, altogether upon the
commonwealth. The common people oweth very many things to thee, but
thou owest all things to them. Though thine ears be compelled to suffer names
of ambition, as most mighty, most christened, holiness, and majesty, yet let thy
mind not be a-knowen of them, but refer all these things unto Christ, to
whom only they agree. Let the crime of treason against thine own person
(which other with great words make an heinous offence) be counted of thee a
very trifle. violateth the majesty of a prince indeed, which in the prince's name
doth any thing cruelly, violently, mischievously, contrary to right. Let no
man's injury move thee less than that which pertaineth to thee privately:
remember thou art a public person, and that thou oughtest not to think but of
common matters. If thou have any courage with thee and readiness of wit,
consider with thyself not how great a man thou art, but how great a charge
thou bearest on thy back: and the more in jeopardy thou art so much the less
favour thyself, fetching example of ministering thine office not of thy predeces-
sors or else of flatterers, of Christ: for what is more unreasonable than that a
christian prince should set before him for an example Hanyball, great Alexan-
dre, Cesar or Pompey, in the which same persons when he cannot attain some
certain virtues, he shall counterfeit those things most chiefly which only were
to be refused and avoided. Let it not forth withal be taken for an example if
Cesar have done anything lauded in histories, but if he have done anything
which varyeth not from the doctrine of our Lord Jesu Christ, or be such that
though it be not worthy to be counterfeited yet may it be applied to the study
or exercise of virtue. Let not an whole empire be of so great value to thee that
thou wouldest wittingly once bow from the right: put off that rather than thou
shouldest put off Christ. Doubt not Christ hath to make thee amends for the
empire refused, far better than the empire. is so comely, so excellent, so glorious unto kings as to draw as nigh as is possible unto the similitude of the
highest king Jesu, as he was the greatest so was he also the best. But that he was

the greatest, that dissimuled he, and hid secret here in earth: that he was the best, that he had liefer we should perceive and feel, because he had liefer we should counterfeit that. He denied his kingdom to be of this world, when he was Lord of heaven and earth also. But the princes of the gentiles use dominion upon them. A christian man exerciseth no power over his but charity, and he which is the chiefest thinketh himself to be minister unto all men, not master or lord. I marvel the more a great deal how these ambitious names of power and dominion were brought in, even unto the very popes and bishops, and that our divines be not ashamed no less indiscreetly than ambitiously to be called everywhere our masters, when Christ forbade his disciples that they should not suffer to be called either lords, or masters: for we must remember that one is in heaven both lord and master Christ Jesus, which is also head unto us all. a shepherd, a bishop, be names of office or service, not of dominion and rule: A pope, an abbot, be names of love, not of power. But why enter I into that great sea of the common errors? Unto whatsoever kind of men he shall turn himself, a very spiritual man shall see many things which he may laugh at, and more which he ought to weep at, he shall see very many opinions so far corrupt and varying from the doctrine of Christ both far and wide: of the which a great part springeth there hence, that we have brought even into Christendom a certain world, and that which is read of the world among the old divines, men of small learning now-a-days refer to them which be not monks. The world in the gospel, with the apostles, with Saint Augustyne, Ambrose, and Hierome, be called infidels, strangers from the faith, the enemies of the cross of Christ. Blasphemers of God, they that are such care for to-morrow and for the time to come, for whosoever mistrusteth Christ neither believe on him, they be they which fight and strive for riches, for rule, for worldly pleasure, as men which, blinded with delyces of sensible things, set their minds and whole affections upon apparent good things, instead of very good things. This world hath not known Christ the very and true light. This world is altogether set on mischief, loveth himself, liveth to himself, studyeth for himself and for his own pleasure, and all for lack he hath not put upon him Christ which is very and true charity. From this world separated Christ not his apostles only, but all men whosoever and as many as he judged worthy of him. After what manner then and fashion I pray you do we mingle with Christendom this world, everywhere in holy scripture condemned? And with the vain name of the world favour, flatter, and maintain our own vices. Many doctors and teachers augment this pestilence, which corrupting the word of God (as Paul saith) wrest and fashion his holy scripture according to the manners of every time, when it were more convenient that the manners should be addressed and amended by the rule of his scripture. And no mischievouser kind of flattering verily is there, than when with the words of the gospel and of the prophets we flatter the diseases of the mind and cure them not. prince heareth all power is of God: forthwith (as the proverb saith) his comb riseth. Why hath the scripture made thee high or swelling in mind rather than circumspect and careful? Thinkest thou that God hath committed to thee an empire to be governed, and thinkest thou not that the same will require of thee a strait reckoning of the ordering thereof? The covetous man heareth it to be forbid unto christian men to have two coats at once. divine interpreteth the second coat to be whatsoever should be superfluous and more than enough for the necessity of nature, and should appertain to the disease of covetousness: that is very well (saith the gross fellow) for I yet lack very many things. natural wise man and cold from charity heareth this to be the order of charity, that thou shouldest regard and set more of thine own money than of another man's, of thine own life than of another man's, of thine own fame than of another man's. I will therefore, saith he, give nothing lest peradventure I should lack myself. I will not defend another man's good fame or good name, lest mine own be spotted thereby. I will forsake my brother in jeopardy, lest I myself should fall in peril also. To speak shortly I will live altogether to myself that no incommodity come to me for any other man's cause. We have also learned if holy men have done anything not to be counterfeited or followed, that only to take of them and draw in to the example of living. Adulterers and murderers flatter and clawen themselves with the example of David. Such as gapeth after worldly riches lay against us for their excuse rich Abraham. Princes which count it but a sport or pastime everywhere to corrupt and defile virgins, number and reckon up to cloke their vice the queens concubines of Salomon. They whose belly is their god, layeth for their excuse the drunkenness of Noe. Incests which pollute their own kinswomen, cloke and cover their filthiness with the example of Loth, which lay with his own daughters. Why turn we our eyes from Christ to these men? dare be bold to say that it ought not to be counterfeited and followed, no not so much as in the prophets or Christ's apostles verily, if anything swerve or wry from the doctrine of Christ. But if it delight men so greatly to counterfeit holy sinners, I do not gainsay them, so that they counterfeit them whole and altogether. Thou hast followed David in adultery, much more follow him in repentance. Thou hast counterfeited Mary Magdalayne a sinner, counterfeit her also loving much, counterfeit her weeping, counterfeit her casting herself down at the feet of Jesu. Thou hast persecuted the church of God as Paul did, thou hast forsworn thyself as Peter did: see likewise that thou stretch forth thy neck for the faith and religion of Christ after the example of Paul, and that thou fear not the cross no more than Peter. For this cause God suffereth even great and right excellent men also to fall into certain vices, that we when we have fallen should not despair, but with this condition, if that we, as we have been their fellows in sinning and doing amiss, even so will be their companions and partners in the amending of our sins and misdeeds. do we greatly praise and magnify that same thing which was not to be counterfeited and followed, and certain things which were well done of them, we do deprave and corrupt, after the manner of spiders sucking out the poison only, if any be therein, or else turning even the wholesome juice also into poison to ourselves. doth Abraham's example belong to thee, which makest of thy money thy God? Because he was enriched with increase of cattle (God making his substance and goods prosperously to multiply) and that in the old law which was but carnal: shall it therefore be lawful to thee which art a christian man, by right or wrong, by hook or crook, from whencesoever it be, heap together riches as much as ever king Cresus had (whose exceeding great riches is come into a common proverb), which riches once gotten thou mightest either evil spend and lewdly waste, or else (which is a great deal worse) hide and bury most covetously deep in the ground? How little Abraham did set his mind upon his goods and riches, which came to him abundantly by their own accord, even this thing may be an evident token and proof, that without delay at the voice of God commanding him, he brought forth his only son to be slain. How much thinkest thou despised he his droves of oxen which despised even his own son? And thinkest thou which dreamest nothing else but of filthy lucre and advantage, which praisest and settest by nothing but only money, which art ready as soon as there chance any hope of lucre, be it never so little, to deceive thy brother, or to set Christ at naught, that there is any similitude or like thing between thee and Abraham? The simple and innocent wenches, the daughters of Loth, when they beheld all the region round about on every part burning and flaming with fire, and supposed that it, which was then in sight afore their eyes, had been all the whole world, and that no man was preserved from that so large and wasteful fire but only themselves, lay privily and by stealth with their own father, not of a filthy but virtuous and holy purpose, that is to wit, lest none issue of mankind should have remained after them, and that, when this precept of God (grow and multiply) was as yet in full vigour and strength. And darest thou compare thy filthy and prodigious voluptuousness and lechery with the deed of these wenches? I would not doubt to count thy matrimony not so good as their incest committed with their father, if in matrimony thou dost not study for issue, but to satisfy thine own voluptuous appetite or lust. after so many excellent and noble examples of virtue and good living shewed, fell once into adultery by occasion and opportunity given him: and shall it be lawful therefore to thee straightway at thy liberty, to roll, welter, and tumble from house to house in other men's beds all thy life long? Peter once for fear of death denied his master Christ, for whose sake afterward he died with good will: Shall it be lawful thinkest thou then to thee for that cause, to forswear thyself for every trifle? Paul sinned not purposely and for the nonce, but fell through ignorance: when he was warned and taught, he repented forthwith and came into the right way. Thou both ware and wise, and seeing what thou doest, wittingly and willingly continuest from youth to age in vices and sins, and yet by the example of Paul strokest thou thine own head. Matthew being commanded but with one word, without any tarrying, at once utterly forsook all his office of receiving custom or tollage: but thou art so sworn and married to thy money that neither so many examples of holy men, neither the gospels of often heard, nor so many preachings can divorce or pluck thee from it. bishops say unto me, Saint Augustyne (as it is read) had two sovereign ladies or concubines: yea but he then was an heathen man, and we be nourished up in Christendom: he was young, and our heads be hoar for age. A worshipful comparison, because that he being young, and also an heathen man, to avoid the snares of matrimony, had a little wench instead of a wife, and yet to her which was not his wife kept he the promise of wedlock. Shall it be therefore the less shame for us christian men being old, being priests, yea being bishops, to be altogether spotted and defiled in every puddle one after another of bodily lusts? Farewell good manners when we have given to vices the names of virtues, and have begun to be more wily and subtle in defending our vices than diligent to amend them, most specially when we have learned to nourish, to underset, and to strengthen our froward opinions, with the help and aid of holy scripture. Thou therefore my most sweet brother (the common people altogether set at naught with their both opinions and deeds) purely and wholly hasten thee unto the christian sect. Whatsoever in this life appeareth to thy sensible powers either to be hated or loved, all that for the love of piety and virtuous life indifferently despised, let Christ only to thee be sufficient, the only author both of true judging and also of blessed living. And this verily the world thinketh to be pure foolishness and madness: nevertheless by this foolishness it pleaseth God to save them which on him believe. And he is happily a fool that is wise in Christ: and he is wofully wise that is foolish in Christ. hearest thou, as I would have thee to vary strongly from the common people, so I would not that thou shewing a point of currishness, shouldst everywhere bark against the opinions and deeds of other men, and with authority condemn them, prattle odiously against all men, furiously preach against the living of every person, lest thou purchase to thyself two evils together. The one that thou shouldest fall into hate of all men: the other that when thou art hated thou shouldest do good to no man. But be thou all things to all men, to win all men to Christ; as much as may be (piety not offended) so shape and fashion thyself to all men outwardly, that within thy purpose remain sure, stedfast and unmoved, withoutforth let gentleness, courteous language, softness, profitableness allure and entice thy brother, whom it is meet with fair means to be induced to Christ, and not to be feared with cruelness. In conclusion that which is in thy breast is not so greatly to be roared forth with cruel words, as to be declared and uttered with honest manners. And again thou oughtest not so to favour the infirmity of the common people that thou durst not at a time strongly defend the verity: with humanity men must be amended, and not deceived.

The seventh rule

CHAPTER XVI

MOREOVER if through infancy and feebleness of mind we cannot as yet attain to these spiritual things, we ought nevertheless to study not the sluggish-er one deal, that at the least we draw as nigh as is possible. How be it the very and compendious way to felicity is, if at once we shall turn our whole mind to the contemplation and beholding of celestial things so fervently, that as the body bringeth with him his shadow, even so the love of Christ, the love of eternal things and honest, bringeth with him naturally the loathsomeness of caduke and transitory things and the hate of filthy things. For either other necessarily followeth the other: and the one with the other either augmenteth or minisheth. As much as thou shalt profit in the love of Christ, so much shalt thou hate the world. The more thou shalt love and set by things invisible, the more vile shall wax things vain and momentary. We must therefore do even that same in the discipline of virtue which Fabius counselleth to be done in sciences or faculties of learning, that we at once press up to the best, which thing yet if through our own fault will not come to pass, the next of all is that we at the least may by certain natural prudence abstain from great vices, and keep ourselves (as much as may be) whole and sound to the beneficence of God. For as that body is near unto health, which (though it be wasted) is free yet and out of the danger of noisome humours, even so is that mind more capax of the benefit of God, is not yet inquynate or defiled with grievous offences, though she lack yet true and perfect virtue. we be too weak to follow the apostles, to follow the martyrs, to follow the virgins, at the least way let us not commit that the Ethnykes or heathen men should seem to over-run us in this plain or lists. Of the which very many when they neither knew God whom they should dread, neither believed any hell whom they should fear: yet deter-mined they that a man ought by all crafts to avoid and eschew filthiness for the thing itself. In so much that many of them chose rather to suffer the loss of fame, loss of goods, in conclusion to suffer loss of life, than to depart from honesty. If sin itself be such a manner thing, that for no commodities or incommodities proffered to man it ought to be committed, certainly if neither the justice of God fear us, neither his beneficence discourage us and move us to the contrary, if no hope of immortality or fear of eternal pain call us aback, or else if the very natural filthiness of sin withdraw us not, which could withdraw the minds of the very gentiles, at the least way let a thousand incommodities which accompany the sinner in this life put a christian man in fear: infamy, loss or waste of goods, poverty, the contempt and hate of good men, grief of mind, unquietness and torment of conscience most miserable of all, which though many feel not now presently, either because they be blinded with dulness of youth, or made drunk with the voluptuousness and pleasure of sin, yet shall they feel it hereafter: and plainly the later it happeneth, so much the more unhappily shall they feel it: wherefore young men most specially should be warned and exhorted that they would rather believe so many authors that the very nature and property of sin were thus indeed than with miserable and woful experience learn it in themselves, and that they would not contaminate nor defile their life before they knew surely what life meant. If Christ be to thee vile, to whom thou art so costly, at the leastway for thine own sake refrain thyself from filthy things. And though it be very perilous to tarry anywhere in this state, as between the ways (as it is in the proverb), nevertheless unto them which cannot as yet climb up to the pure, perfect and excellent virtue, it shall not be a little profitable to be in the civil or moral virtues rather than to run headlong in to all kind of vices and uncleanliness. is not the resting place and quiet haven of felicity, but from hence is a shorter journey and an easier stair up to felicity. In the mean season for all that, we must pray God that he will vouchsafe to pluck us up to better things.

The eighth rule

CHAPTER XVII

IF the storm of temptation shall rise against thee somewhat thick and grievously, begin not forthwithal to be discontent with thyself, as though for that cause God either cared not for thee, or favoured thee not, or that thou shouldest be but an easy christian man, or else the less perfect: but rather give thanks to God because he instructeth thee as one which shall be his heir in time to come, because he beateth or scourgeth thee as his most singular beloved son and proveth thee as his assured friend. It is a very great token a man to be reject from the mercy of God when he is vexed with no temptations. Let come to thy mind the apostle Paul which obtained to be admitted or let in even in to the mysteries of the third heaven, yet was he beaten of the angel of Satan. come to remembrance the friend of God, Job: remember Jerom, Benedict, Frauncys, and with these innumerable other holy fathers, vexed and troubled of very great vices: if that which thou sufferest be common to so great men, be common to so many men as well as to thee, what cause is there wherefore thou shouldest be smit out of countenance, shouldest be abashed or fall into despair? Enforce rather and strive that thou mayst overcome as they did, God shall not forsake thee, but with temptation shall make increase, that thou mayst be able to endure.

The ninth rule

CHAPTER XVIII

AS expert captains are wont to cause, when all things are quiet, at rest and at peace, that the watch nevertheless be duly kept: see thou that thou have alway thy mind watching and circumspect against the sudden assault of thine enemy (for he ever compasseth round about seeking whom he might devour) that thou mayst be the more ready as soon as he assaulteth thee to put him back manfully, to confound him and forthwith to tread underfoot the head of the pestiferous and poison serpent: he is never overcome either more easily or more surely and perfectly, than by that means. Therefore it is a very wise point to dash the young children of Babylon (as soon as they be born) against the stone which is Christ, or they grow strong and great.

The tenth rule

CHAPTER XIX

BUT the tempter is put back most of all by this means, if thou shalt either vehemently hate, abhor and defy, and in a manner spit at him straightway whensoever he enticeth and moveth thee with any temptation, or else if thou pray fervently or get thyself to some holy occupation, setting thine whole mind thereunto: or if thou make answer to the tempter with words set out of holy scripture, as I have warned thee before. In which thing verily it shall not profit meanly against all kind of temptation to have some certain sentences prepared and ready, specially those with which thou hast felt thy mind to be moved and stirred vehemently.

The eleventh rule

CHAPTER XX

TWO dangers chiefly follow good men, one lest in temptation they give up their hold. Another lest after the victory in their consolation and spiritual joy they wax wanton and stand in their own conceit, or else please themselves. Therefore that thou mayst be sure not only from the night fear, but also from the devil of mid-day: when thine enemy stirreth thee unto filthy things that thou behold not thine own feebleness or weakness, but remember only that thou canst do all things in Christ, said not to his apostles only, but to thee also and to all his members, even unto the very lowest: Have confidence for I have overcome the world. Again whensoever either after thine enemy is overcome, or in doing some holy work, thou shalt feel thy mind inwardly to be comforted with certain privy delectations: then beware diligently that thou ascribe nothing thereof unto thine own merits, but thank only the free beneficence of God for altogether, and hold down and refrain thyself with the words of Paul, saying: What hast thou, that thou hast not received? If thou have received it, why rejoicest thou as though thou haddest not received it? And so against this double mischief shall there be a double remedy, if thou in the conflict mistrusting thine own strength dost flee for succour unto thy head Christ, putting the whole trust of conquering in the benevolence of him only. And if also in the spiritual comfort and consolation, thou immediately give thanks to him for his benefit, humbly knowing and confessing thine unworthiness.

The twelfth rule

CHAPTER XXI

WHEN thou fightest with thine enemies, think it not enough for thee to avoid his stroke, or put it back, except thou also take the weapon from him manfully, and lay therewith again at the owner, killing him with his own sword. That shall come to pass on this wise. when thou art provoked unto evil thou do not only abstain from sin, but thereof dost take unto thee an occasion of virtue: and as poets elegantly feign that Hercules did grow and was also hardened in courage through the dangers that Juno put unto him of displeasure: thou likewise give also attendance that by the instigations of thine enemy not only thou be not the worse but rather be made much better. Thou art stirred unto bodily lust, know thy weakness, and also lay apart somewhat the more of lawful pleasures, and add some increase unto chaste and holy occupations. Thou art pricked unto covetousness and nyggysshe keeping: increase alms deeds. Thou art moved unto vain glory: so much the more humble thyself in all things. thus shall it be brought about that every temptation may be a certain renewing of thy holy purpose, and an increase of piety and virtuous living. And verily other means is there none at all of so great virtue and strength to vanquish and overthrow our enemy: for he shall be afraid to provoke thee afresh, lest he which rejoiceth to be the beginner and chief captain of wickedness should minister an occasion of piety, virtue and godliness.

The thirteenth rule

CHAPTER XXII

BUT alway take heed that thou fight with this mind and hope, as though that should be the last fight that ever thou shalt have, if thou get the over hand: for it may be verily that the benignity of God will give and grant this reward unto thy virtue and noble act: that thine enemy once overcome to his shame, shall never afterward come upon thee again. A thing which we read to have happened to divers holy men: neither believeth Origene against reason, that when christian men overcome, then is the power of their enemies minished, whiles the adversary once put back manfully is never suffered to return again to make a fresh battle. Be bold therefore in the conflict, to hope for perpetual peace. again after thou hast overcome, so behave thyself as though thou shouldest go again to fight straightway, for after one temptation, we must look ever for another: we may never depart from our harness and weapons: we may never forsake our standing: we may never leave off watch as long as we war in the garrison of this body. Every man must have alway that saying of the prophet in his heart, I will keep my standing.

The fourteenth rule

CHAPTER XXIII

WE must take very good heed that we despise not any vice as light, for no enemy over cometh oftener than he which is not set off: in which thing I perceive not a few men to be greatly deceived: for they deceive themselves while they favour themselves in one or two vices, every man after his own appetite thinketh to be venial, and all other grievously abhor. A great part of them which the common people call perfect and uncorrupt, greatly defieth theft, extortion, murder, adultery, incest: but single fornication and moderate use of voluptuous pleasures as a small trespass, they refuse not all. Some one man being unto all other things uncorrupt enough is somewhat a good drinker, is in riot and expenses somewhat wasteful. Another is somewhat liberal of his tongue. Another is cumbered with vanity, vainglory and boasting. At the last, what vice shall we lack if every man after this manner shall favour his own vice? i is an evident token that those men which favour any vice at all should not truly possess the other virtues but rather some images of virtues which either nature or bringing up, finally very custom, hath grafted in the minds of the very gentiles. But he, which with christian hatred abhorreth any one vice, must needs abhor all: for he whose mind true charity hath once possessed hateth indifferently the whole host of evil things, and flattereth not himself so much as in venial sins, lest he might fall a little and a little from the smallest to the greatest: and while he is negligent in light things might fall from the chiefest things of all. though thou as yet canst not pluck up by the roots the whole generation of vices: nevertheless somewhat of our evil properties must be plucked away day by day, and something added to good manners: after that manner diminisheth or augmenteth the great heap of Hesiodus.

The fifteenth rule

CHAPTER XXIV

IF the labour which thou must take in the conflict of temptation shall fear thee, this shall be a remedy. See thou compare not the grief of the fight with the pleasure of the sin: but match me the present bitterness of the fight with the bitterness of the sin hereafter which followeth him that is overthrown: then set the present sweetness of the sin which enticeth thee, with the pleasure of the victory hereafter, and with the tranquillity of mind which followeth him that fighteth lustily: and anon thou shalt perceive how unequal a comparison there shall be. But in this thing they which be but little circumspect are deceived, because they compare the displeasure of the fight with the pleasure of the sin, and consider not what followeth the one and the other. For there followeth him which is overcome, grief both more painful a great deal and also of longer continuance than he should have had in time of fight, if he had won the victory. And likewise there followeth the conquerors more pleasure by a great deal and of longer endurance than was the pleasure which carried him into sin that was overcome: which thing he shall lightly judge, that hath had the proof of both. But no man that is christened ought to be so outright a coward though he were daily subdued of temptation, that he should once at the least do his endeavour to prove what thing it is to overcome temptation, which thing the oftener he shall do, the pleasanter shall the victory be made unto him.

The sixteenth rule

CHAPTER XXV

BUT if at any time it shall fortune thee to receive a deadly wound, beware lest by and by (thy shield cast away and weapons forsaken) thou yield thyself to thine enemies' hands, which thing I have perceived to happen unto many, whose minds naturally are somewhat feeble and soft without resistance, after they were once overthrown, they ceased to wrestle any more, but permitted and gave themselves altogether unto affections, never thinking any more to recover their liberty again. Too too much perilous is this weakness of spirit, which now and then though it be not coupled with the most wits in the world, yet is it wont to bring to that point which is worst of all, to desperation verily. Against this weakness therefore thy mind must be aforehand armed with this rule, that after we have fallen into sin not only we should not despair, but counterfeit bold men of war, whom not seldom shame of rebuke and grief of the wound received not only putteth not to flight but sharpeneth and refresheth again to fight more fiercely than they did before. like case also after that we have been brought in to deadly sin, let us haste anon to come again to ourselves and to take a good heart to us, and to repair again the rebuke and shame of the fall with new courage and lustiness of strength. Thou shalt heal one wound sooner than many: thou shalt easier cure a fresh wound than that which is now old and putrefied. Comfort thyself with that famous verse which Demostenes is said to have used: A man that fleeth will yet fight again. Call to remembrance David the prophet, Salomon the king, Peter a captain of the church, Paul the apostle, so great lights of holiness: into what great sins for all that fell they? Which all peradventure even for this cause God suffered to fall, lest thou when thou haddest fallen shouldest despair: rise up again therefore upon thy feet but that quickly and with a lusty courage, and go to it afresh, both fiercer and also more circumspect. It happeneth sometime that deadly offences grow to good men into a heap of virtuous living, while they love more fervently which erred most shamefully.

The seventeenth rule

CHAPTER XXVI

BUT against sundry and diverse assaults of the tempter thine enemy, sundry and diverse remedies are very meet and convenient. Nevertheless the only and chief remedy which of all remedies is of most efficacy and strength against all kinds either of adversity or else temptation is the cross of Christ. which self-same is both an example to them that go out of the way, and a refreshing to them that labour, and also armour or harness to them that fight. This is a thing to be cast against all manner weapons and darts of our most wicked enemy. And therefore it is necessary to be exercised diligently therein, not after the common manner, as some men repeat daily the history of the passion of Christ, or honour the image of the cross, or with a thousand signs of it arm all their body round on every side, or keep some piece of that holy tree laid up at home in their house, or at certain hours so call to remembrance Christ's punishment, that they may have compassion and weep for him with natural affection, as they would for a man that is very just and suffereth great wrong unworthily. is not the true fruit of that tree: nevertheless let it in the mean season be the milk of the souls which be younglings and weak in Christ. But climb thou up into the date tree, that is to say the tree of victory, that thou mayest take hold of the true fruits thereof. These be the chief if we, which be members, shall endeavour ourselves to be semblable unto our head in mortifying our affections, which be our members upon the earth, which thing unto us ought only to be nothing bitter, but also very pleasant and fervently to be desired, if so be the spirit of Christ live in us. For who loveth truly and heartily that person to whom he rejoiceth to be as unlike as may be, and in living and conversation clean contrary? Notwithstanding that thou mayest the more profit, in thy mind record the mystery of the cross. It shall behoveful that every man prepare unto himself a certain way and godly craft of fighting and therein diligently exercise, that as soon as need shall require it may be ready at hand.

Such may the craft be, that in certifying of every thine affections thou mayest apply that part of the cross which most specially thereto agreeth: for there is not at all any either temptation, either adversity, which hath not his proper remedy in the cross. when thou art tickled with ambition of this world, when thou art ashamed to be had in derision and to be set at naught: consider thou then, most vile member, great Christ thy head is, and unto what vileness he humbled himself for thy sake. When the evil of envy invadeth thy mind, remember how kindly, how lovingly he bestowed himself every whit unto our use and profit, how good he is even unto the worst. When thou art moved with gluttony, have in mind how he drank gall with eysell. When thou art tempted with filthy pleasure, call to remembrance how far from all manner of pleasure the whole life of thy head was, and how full of incommodities, vexation, and grief. When ire provoketh thee, let him come immediately to thy mind, which like a lamb before the shearer held his peace and opened not his mouth. If poverty wring thee evil, or covetousness disquiet thee, anon let him be rolled in thy mind that is the Lord of all things, and yet was made so poor and needy for thy sake that he had not whereupon to rest his head. And after the same manner if thou shalt do in all other temptations also, not only it shall not be grievous to have oppressed thine affections, but surely pleasant and delectable, for because thou shalt perceive that thou by this means art conformed and shapen like unto thy head, and that thou dost as it were recompense him for his infinite sorrows, which for thy sake he suffered unto the uttermost.

The eighteenth rule

CHAPTER XXVII

AND verily this manner of remedy, though it alone of all remedies be most present and ready, most sure and quick in working to them which be meanly entered in the way of living, nevertheless to the weaker sort these things also shall somewhat profit: when affection moveth unto iniquity, then at once they call before the eyes of the mind how filthy, how abominable, how mischievous a thing sin is: on the other side how great is the dignity of man. In trifles and matters such as skilleth not if all the world knew, we take some deliberation and advisement with ourselves. In this matter of all matters most weighty and worthy to be pondered, before that with consent as with our own hand writing we bind ourselves to the fiend, shall we not reckon and account with our mind of how noble a craftsman we were made, in how excellent estate we are set, with how exceeding great price we are bought, unto how great felicity we are called, and that man is that gentle and noble creature for whose sake only God hath forged the marvellous building of this world, that he is of the company of angels, the son of God, the heir of immortality, a member of Christ, a member of the church, that our bodies be the temple of the Holy Ghost, our minds the images and also the secret habitations of the deity. And on the other side that sin is the most filthy pestilence and consumption both of the mind and of the body also, for both of them through innocency springeth anew into their own natural kind, and through contagion of sin both putrefy and rot even in this world. Sin is that deadly poison of the most filthy serpent, the prest wages of the devil, and of that service which is not most filthy only, but also most miserable. After thou hast considered this and such like with thyself, ponder wisely and take sure advisement and deliberation whether it should be wisely done or no, for an apparent momentary and poisoned little short pleasure of sin, to fall from so great dignity into so vile and wretched estate, from whence thou canst not rid and deliver thyself by thine own power and help.

The nineteenth rule

CHAPTER XXVIII

FURTHERMORE compare together those two captains by themselves most contrary and unlike, God and the devil, of which the one thou makest thine enemy when thou sinnest, and the other thy lord and master. Through innocency and grace thou art called in to the number of the friends of God, art elect unto the right title and inheritance of the sons of God. By sin verily thou art made both the bond servant and son of the devil. one of them is that eternal fountain and original patron and true example of very and sure beauty, of very true pleasure, of most perfect goodness, ministering himself to all things. The other is father of all mischief, of extreme filthiness, of uttermost infelicity. Remember the benefits and goodness of the one done to thee, and the evil deeds of the other. With what goodness hath the one made thee? With what mercy redeemed thee? With what liberty and freedom endued thee? With what tenderness daily suffereth he and sustaineth thee, a wretched sinner, patiently abiding and looking for amendment? With what joy and gladness doth he receive thee amended, and when thou art come again to thyself? Contrary to all these things with how natural hate and envy long ago did the devil lay wait to thy health? Into what grievous and cumbrous vexation hath he cast thee, and also what other thing imagineth he daily but to draw all mankind with him into eternal mischief? All these things on this side and that side, well and substantially weighed and pondered, thus think with thyself: shall I unmindful of mine original beginning from whence I came, unmindful of so great and manifold benefits, for so small a morsel of feigned and false pleasure, unkindly depart from so noble, from so loving, from so beneficial a father, and shall mancipate and make myself bond willingly unto a most filthy and a most cruel master? Shall I not at the least way make good to the one that thing which I would perform to a vile man, which had shewed kindness, or done me any good? Shall I not fly from the other, which would fly from a man that coveted or were about to do me hurt?

The twentieth rule

CHAPTER XXIX

AND verily the rewards be no less unequal than the captains and givers of them be contrary and unlike. what is more unequal than eternal death and immortal life? Than without end to enjoy everlasting felicity and blessedness, in the company and fellowship of the heavenly citizens, and without end to be tormented and punished with extreme vengeance, in the most unhappy and wretched company of damned souls? And whosoever doubteth of this thing, he is not so much as a man verily, and therefore he is no christian man. And whosoever thinketh not on this, nor hath it in remembrance, is even madder than madness itself. and besides all this, virtue and wickedness hath in the mean season even in this life their fruits very much unlike, for of the one is reaped assured tranquillity and quietness of mind, and that blessed joy of pure and clean conscience, which joy, whosoever shall once have tasted, there is nothing in all this world so precious nor nothing so pleasant, wherewith he would be glad or desirous to change it. Contrariwise there followeth the other, that is to say wickedness, a thousand other evils, but most specially that most wretched torment and vexation of unclean conscience. That is that hundred-fold reward of spiritual joy which Christ promised in the gospel, as a certain earnest or taste of eternal felicity. These be those marvellous rewards that the apostle speaketh of which eye neither saw nor ear hath heard, neither hath sunk into the heart of any man, which God hath prepared for them that love him, and verily in this life, when in the mean season the worm of wicked men dieth not, they suffer their hell pains here even in this world. Neither any other thing is that flame in which is tormented the rich glutton of whom is made mention in the gospel: neither any other things be those punishments of them in hell of whom the poets write so many things, save a perpetual grief, unquietness or gnawing of the mind which accompanieth the custom of sin. He that will therefore, let him set aside the reward of the life to come, which be so diverse and unlike: yet in this life virtue hath annexed to her wherefore she abundantly ought to be desired, and vice hath coupled unto him for whose sake he ought to be abhorred.

The twenty-first rule

CHAPTER XXX

MOREOVER consider how full of grief and misery, how short and transitory is this present life, how on every side death lieth in await against us, how everywhere he catcheth us suddenly and unaware. And when no man is sure, no not of one moment of life, how great peril it is to prolong and continue that kind of life in which (as it often fortuneth) if sudden death should take thee thou were but lost and undone for ever.

The twenty-second rule

CHAPTER XXXI

BESIDES all this impenitency or obduration of mind is to be feared of all mischiefs the extreme and worst: namely if a man would ponder this one thing of so many, how few there be which truly and with all their hearts come to themselves again, and be clean converted from sin, and with due repentance reconciled to God again: specially of them which have drawn along the lives of iniquity even unto the last end of their life. verily and easy is the fall or descent into filthiness, but to return back again there-hence, and to scape up unto spiritual light, this is a work, this is a labour. Therefore at the leastway thou being monished and warned by the chance of Esope's goat, before thou descend into the pit of sin, remember that there is not so easy coming back again.

Remedies against certain sins and special
vices, and first against bodily lust

CHAPTER XXXII

HITHERTO have we verily opened and declared (howsoever it be done)
common remedies against all kind of vices. Now we shall assay to give also
certain special and particular remedies, how and by what means thou oughtest
withstand every vice and sin, and first of all how thou mayst resist the lust of
the body. Than the which evil there is none other that sooner invadeth us,
neither sharper assaileth or vexeth us, nor extendeth larger nor draweth more
unto their utter destruction. If at any time therefore filthy lust shall stir thy
mind, with these weapons and armour remember forthwith to meet him: first
think how uncleanly, how filthy, how unworthy for any man whatsoever he be
that pleasure is which assimuleth and maketh us, that be a divine work, equal
not to beasts only, but also unto filthy swine, to goats, to dogs, and of all brute
beasts, unto the most brute, yea which farther forth casteth down far under the
condition and state of beasts, us which be appointed unto the company of
angels and fellowship of the deity. come to thy mind also how momentary the
same is, how impure, how ever having more aloes than of honey. on the contrary side how noble a thing the soul is, how worshipful a thing the body of a
man is, as I have rehearsed in the rules above. What the devil's peevishness is it
that for so little, so uncleanly tickling of momentary pleasures to defile at one
time both soul and body with ungodly manners? To profane and pollute that
temple which Christ hath consecrate to himself with his blood? that also what
an heap of mischievous incommodities that flattering pleasant pestilence
bringeth with him. First of all it pulleth from thee thy good fame, a possession
far-away most precious, for the rumour of no vice stinketh more carenly than
the name of lechery: it consumeth thy patrimony, it killeth at once both the
strength and also the beauty of the body, it decayeth and greatly hurteth
health, it engendereth diseases innumerable and them filthy, it disfigureth the

flower of youth long before the day, it hasteth or accelerateth reviled and evil favoured age, it taketh away the quickness and strength of the wit, it dulleth the sight of the mind, and grafteth in a man as it were a beastly mind, it withdraweth at once from all honest studies and pastimes, and plungeth and souseth a man every-whit in the puddle and mire be he never so excellent, that now he hath lust to think on nothing but that which is sluttish, vile, and filthy: and it taketh away the use of reason which was the native property of man, it maketh youth mad, peevish, and slanderous, and age odious, filthy, and wretched. Be wise therefore and on this wise reckon with thyself name by name, this and that pleasure came so evil to pass, brought with her so much loss, so much disworship, dishonour and dishonesty, so much tediousness, labour and disease: and shall I now, a fool most natural, devour that hook wittingly? Shall I again commit that thing whereof I should repent of fresh? likewise refrain thyself by the example of other men, which thou hast known to have followed voluptuous pleasures filthily and unfortunately. On the other side courage and bold thyself unto chastity by the examples of so many young men, of so many young and tender virgins nourished up delicately and in pleasures: And (the circumstances compared together) lay against thyself thy sluggishness, why thou at the last should not be able to do that thing which such and such, of that kind or sex, of that age, so born, so brought up were and yet be able to do? Love as much as they did, and thou shalt be able to do no less than they did. Think how honest, how pleasant, how lusty and flourishing a thing is pureness of body and of mind, the most of all maketh us acquainted and familiar with angels, and apt to receive the Holy Ghost: for verily that noble spirit, the lover of pureness, so greatly fleeth back from no vice at all as from uncleanliness, he resteth and sporteth him nowhere so much as in pure virgins' minds. before thine eyes how ungodly it is, how altogether a mad thing to love, to wax pale, to be made lean, to weep, to flatter, and shamefully to submit thyself unto a stinking harlot most filthy and rotten, to gape and sing all night at her chamber window, to be made to the lure and be obedient at a beck, nor dare do anything except she nod or wag her head, to suffer a foolish woman to reign over thee, to chide thee: to lay unkindness one against the other, to fall out, to be made at one again, to give thyself willing unto a quean, that she might mock, kocke, mangle and spoil thee. Where is, I beseech thee, among all these things the name of a man? Where is thy beard? Where is that noble mind created unto most beautiful and noble things? Consider also another thing with thyself, how great a flock of mischiefs voluptuousness (if she be let in) is wont to bring with her. Other vices peradventure have some acquaintance with certain virtues, filthy lust hath none at all, but is annexed and alway coupled with those sins that be greatest and most in number. Let it be but a trifle or a light matter to follow queans, yet is it a grievous thing not to regard thy father and mother, to set at naught thy friends, to consume thy father's good in waste, to pluck away from other men, to forswear thyself, to drink all night, to rob, to use witchcraft, to fight, to commit murder, to blaspheme. Into which all and grievouser than these, the lady pleasure will draw thee headlong, after thou once hast ceased to be thine own man, and hast put thy wretched head under her girdle. Ponder moreover how this life vanisheth away faster than smoke, less of substance than a shadow, and how many snares death pitcheth for us, laying await in every place and at all seasons. and at this point it shall profit singularly, to call to remembrance and that name by name, if that sudden death hath taken away any sometime of thine acquaintance, of thy familiar friends, of thy companions, or else of them which were younger than thou: and most specially of them which in time passed thou hast had fellows of filthy pastime. And learn of another man's peril to be more ware and circumspect. Remember how deliciously they lived, but how bitterly they departed: how late they waxed wise, how late they began to hate their mortiferous and deadly pleasures. come to remembrance the sharpness of the extreme judgment, and the terrible lightning of that fearful sentence never to be revoked, sending wicked men into eternal fire, and that this pleasure of an hour, short and little, must be punished with eternal torments. In this place weigh diligently in a pair of balances, how unequal a change it is for the most filthy and very short delectation of lust, both to lose in this life the joy of the mind, much sweeter and more excellent, and in the life to come to be spoiled of joys everlasting. Moreover with so shadow-like and little vain pleasure to purchase sorrows never to be ended. Finally if it seem a hard thing to despise that so small delectation for Christ's sake, remember what pains he took upon him for the tender love he bare to thee. And beside the common injuries of man's life, how much of his holy blood shed he, how shameful, how bitter death suffered he, and all for thee. And thou of all those things unmindful crucifiest again the son of God, iterating afresh those mad pleasures which caused and compelled thy head and lord unto so cruel torments. Then according to the rule above rehearsed, call to mind how much of benefits he heaped on thee, as yet thou haddest deserved nothing at all: for the which although no sufficient or like recompense can be made of thy part for the least, yet desireth he again none other thank but that thou, after his example, shouldest refrain thy mind from deadly and mortal pleasures, and turn thee unto the love of infinite goodness and of infinite pleasures and beauty. together these two, Venus and two Cupydes of Plato, that is to say honest love and filthy love, holy pleasure and uncleanly pastime, together the unlike matter of either other. the natures, compare the rewards: and in all temptations, but namely when thou art stirred to filthy lust, set to thee before thine eyes thy good angel, which is thy keeper and continual beholder and witness of all things thou doest or thinkest, and God ever looking on, unto whose eyes all things are open, which sitteth above the heavens and beholdeth the secret places of the earth: and wilt not thou be afraid before the angel present and even hard by thee, before God, and all the company of heaven looking on and abhorring, to commit a thing so abominable and filthy that it would shame thee to do the same thing in the presence of one vile man? This thing I wouldest thou shouldest think as it is indeed. And if it were so that thou haddest eyes much sharper of sight than hath a beast called lynx, much clearer than hath the eagle, yet with these eyes in the most clearest light that could be, couldest thou not behold more surely that thing which a man doeth before thee, than all the privy and secret parts of thy mind be open unto the sight of God and of his angels. also count in thy mind when thou art overcome of bodily lust, of two things the one must follow, either that voluptuousness, once tasted, so shall enchant and darken thy mind, that thou must go from filthiness to filthiness, until thou clean blinded shall be brought in sensum reprobum, that is to say, into a lewd and reproved judgment: and so, made obstinate and sturdy in evil, canst not, no truly not then, yield up filthy pleasure when she hath forsaken thee, which thing we see to have happened to very many, that when the body is wasted, when beauty is withered and vanished, when the blood is cold, when strength faileth, and the eyes wax dim, yet still continually they itch without ceasing. And with greater mischief are now filthy speakers than before time, they have been unshameful livers, than which thing what can be more abominable and monstrous? The other is, if peradventure it shall happen thee by the special favour of God to come again to thyself. Then must that short and fugitive pleasure be purged with very great sorrow of mind, with mighty and strong labour, with continual streams of tears: how much more wisdom therefore is it not to receive at all the poison of carnal pleasure, than either to be brought into so uncurable blindness, or else to recompense so little, and that also false pleasure, with so great grievance and dolorous pain. Moreover thou mayst take many things of the circumstance of thine own person, which might call thee back from voluptuous pleasure. art a priest, remember that thou art altogether consecrate to things pertaining unto God: what a mischievous deed, how ungoodly, how unmeet, and how unworthy it should be to touch the rotten and stinking flesh of an whore with that mouth wherewith thou receivest that precious body so greatly to be honoured, and to handle loathsome and abominable filth with the same hands wherewithal (even the angels ministering to thee and assisting thee) thou executest that ineffable and incomprehensible mystery. Now these things agree not, to be made one body and one spirit with God, and to be made one body with an whore. thou be learned, so much the nobler and liker unto God is thy mind, and so much the more unworthy of this shame and rebuke. thou be a gentleman, if thou be a prince, the more aperte and open the abomination is: the grievouser occasion giveth it unto other inferiors to follow the same. thou be married, remember what an honest thing is a bed undefiled. And give diligence (as much as infirmity shall suffer) that thy wedlock may counterfeit the most holy marriage of Christ and his church, whose image it beareth: that is to wit, that thy marriage may be clean barren in uncleanliness, and plenteous in procreation: for in no kind of living can it be but very filthy to serve and be bound to uncleanly lusts. thou be a young man, take good heed busily that thou pollute not unadvisedly the flower of thy youth, which shall never spring again: and that thou cast not away upon a thing most filthy thy best and very golden years, which flee away most swiftly, and never return again: beware also lest now through the ignorance and negligence of youth, thou commit that thing which should grudge thee hereafter by all thy whole life, conscience of thy misdeeds ever persecuting thee with those his most bitter, most grievous and sharp stings, which when pleasure departeth she leaveth behind her in our minds. thou be a woman, this kind nothing more becometh than chastity, than shame, and fear of dishonesty. thou be a man, so much the more art thou meet and worthy of greater things, and unmeet and unworthy of these so lewd things. thou be old, wish thou haddest some other man's eyes to behold thyself withal, that thou mightest see how evil voluptuousness should become thee, which in youth verily is miserable and to be bridled, but in an old fool verily wonderful and monstrous, and also even unto the very followers of pleasure, a jesting and mocking stock. Among all monsters none is more wonderful than filthy lust in age. dotypol, oh too much forgetful of thyself: at the least way behold at a glass the hoar hairs and white snow of thy head, thy forehead furrowed with wrinkles, and thy carrion face most like unto a dead corpse: now at the last end when thou art come even unto the pit's brink care for other things more agreeable unto thy years: at the leastway that which became thee to have done before time (reason moving thee) do now, thy years putting thee in remembrance or rather compelling thee. Even now pleasure herself casteth thee off, saying, neither I now am comely unto thee, neither yet thou meet or apt unto me. Thou hast played enough, thou hast eaten enough, thou hast drunk enough, it is time for thee to depart, why holdest thou yet so fast and art so greedy on pleasures of this life, when very life herself forsaketh thee. Now it is time for that mystical concubine Abysac that once she may begin to rest in thy bosom, let her with holy rage of love heat thy mind, and with the embracings of her keep thee warm and comfort thy cold members.

A short recapitulation of remedies against the flame of lust

CHAPTER XXXIII

FINALLY to make a short and compendious conclusion, these be the most special things which will make thee sure from pleasures and enticings of the flesh, first of all, circumspect and diligent avoiding of all occasions, precept though it be meet to be observed also in other things, because that he which loveth perils is worthy to perish therein, yet these be most chiefly those Syrenes which almost never man at all hath escaped, he which hath kept far off. Secondly, moderation of eating and drinking and of sleep, temperance and abstinence from pleasures, yea from such as be lawful and permitted: the regard of thine own death, and the contemplation of the death of Christ, and those things also will help if thou shalt live with such as be chaste and uncorrupted: if thou shalt eschew as a certain pestilence the communication of corrupt and wanton persons: if thou shalt flee idle solitariness and sluggish idleness: if thou shalt exercise thy mind strongly in the meditation of celestial things, and in honest studies. But specially if thou shalt consecrate thyself with all thy might unto the investigation or searching of mysteries of holy scripture: if thou shalt pray both oft and purely, most of all when temptation invadeth and assaulteth thee.

Against the enticings and provokings unto avarice

CHAPTER XXXIV

IF thou shalt perceive that thou art either by nature anything inclined to the vice of avarice, or stirred by the devil: call to remembrance (according, to the rules above rehearsed) the dignity of thy condition or state, which for this thing only wast created, for this redeemed, that thou ever shouldest enjoy that infinite good thing God, for God hath forged all the whole building of this world that all things should obey unto thy use and necessity. How filthy then and of how strait and narrow a mind is it, not to use but so greatly to wonder at things dumb and most vile: take away the error of men, what shall gold and silver be but red earth and white? Shalt thou be the disciple of poor Christ and, called to a better possession, wonder at that as a certain great and excellent thing which no philosopher of the gentiles did not set at naught? to possess riches, but to despise riches, is a noble thing. But the commonalty of christian men by name only cry out against me, and be glad to deceive themselves most craftily: very necessity (say they) compelleth us to gather good together, whereof if there should be none at all, then could we not once live verily: if it should be thin and poor, then should we live in much misery without pleasure. But and if it be somewhat clean and honest, and somewhat plenteous withal, it bringeth many commodities to man. The good liking of body is well seen unto, provision is made for our children, we lend and profit our friends, we are delivered from contempt and be the more set by: in conclusion also a man shall have the better name when he is somewhat wealthy. Of a great many thousands of christian men thou canst scarce find one or two that doth not both say and think the same. Nevertheless to answer these men unto both parts. of all because they cloak their covetousness with the name of necessity, I will lay against them the parable rehearsed in the gospel of the lilies and of the birds living from day to day without farther provision, whose example Christ exhorteth us to counterfeit. I will lay against them that the same Christ would not once suffer so much as a scrip to be carried about of his disciples. I will lay against them, that he commandeth us (all other things laid apart) before all things to seek the kingdom of heaven, and promiseth that all things shall be cast and given to us. When at any time had not they things necessary to maintain life withal sufficiently, which with all their hearts have given themselves to virtue and to the true life of a christian man? And how small a thing is that which nature requireth of us? But thou measurest necessity not by the needs of nature, but by the bounds of covetousness. But unto good men even that is enough that scarcely contenteth nature. verily I do not so greatly set of these which forsake at one chop their whole substance every whit that they might the more shamefully beg of other. It is none offence to possess money, but to love and set store by money that is a vice and cousin to sin. If riches flow unto thee, use the office of a good dispenser: but and if it ebb and go away, be not consumed with thought, as though thou were robbed of a greater thing, but rather rejoice that thou art delivered of a perilous fardel. Notwithstanding he which consumeth the chief study and pastime of his life in heaping up riches together, which gapeth at them as a certain excellent or noble thing, and highly to be desired, and layeth them up in store, that he may have enough to serve him for long time, yea though he should live even to the age of Nestor: man peradventure may well be called a good merchant, but verily I would not say that he were a very good christian man, that hangeth all together of himself, and hath distrust of the promises of Christ, whose goodness, it is easy to wit, shall not fail a good man putting his trust in him, seeing that he so liberally both feedeth and clotheth the poor sparrows. But let us now cast accounts of the commodities, which riches is believed to bring with him. First of all even by the common consent of the gentile philosophers: among the good things which are called bona utilia, that is to say, good profitable things, hath the lowest place. And when all other things (after the division of Epictetus) are without man, except only virtue of the mind: yet nothing is so much without us as money is, nothing bringeth so little commodity. whatsoever there is anywhere of gold, whatsoever there is of precious stones, if thou alone hadst it every deal in thy possession, shall thy mind be therefore the better by the value of one hair? Shalt thou be the wiser? Shalt thou be the cunninger? Shalt thou be any whit the more in good health of body? Shall it make thee more strong and lusty? More fair and beauteous? More young? No, truly. But you will say that it purchaseth pleasures, truth it is: but they be deadly pleasures; it getteth a man honour: but what honour I pray you? false honour, which they give, that prayeth nothing, setteth by nothing but only foolish things, and of whom to be praised, is well near to be dispraised. True honour is to be lauded of them which are commendable and praiseworthy themselves. The highest honour that can be is to have pleased Christ. honour is the reward, not of riches, but of virtue. The foolish people giveth thee room and place, gazeth upon thee, and giveth thee honour and reverence. Oh fool, they wonder at thine apparel, and honoureth it, and not thee: Why dost thou not descend into thine own conscience, and consider the miserable poverty of thy mind? Which if the common people saw, then would they judge thee as miserable and wretched, as they now call thee happy and blessed. But good getteth friends. I grant, but yet feigned and false friends: neither getteth it friends to thee but to itself. And certainly the rich man is in this point of all men most unfortunate and wretched, because he cannot so much as discern or know his true friends and lovers from other. One hateth him privily and secretly in heart and mind as an hard niggard. hath envy at him, because he passeth him in riches. Another looking to his own profit and advantage flattereth him, and holdeth up his yea and his nay, and smileth upon him, to the end that he may scrape and get something from him. He that before his face is most loving and kind wisheth and prayeth for his quick and hasty death. There is none that loveth him so heartily and entirely, but that he had liefer have him dead than alive. No man is so familiar with him, that he will tell him the truth. But be it in case there were one special friend among a thousand that loved a rich man heartily without any manner of feigning, yet cannot the rich man but have in suspicion and mistrust every man. He judgeth all men to be vultures and ravenous birds gaping for carrion: he thinketh all men to be flies flying to him, to suck out some profit of him for themselves. Whatsoever commodity therefore riches seemeth to bring, it for the most part, or else altogether is but coloured and deceitful, it is shadow-like and full of delusion, appearing otherwise than it is in very deed. But they bring very many things which are evil indeed, and taketh away very many of these things which are good in very deed. Therefore if thou wilt lay accounts well and perfectly of that which is won, and that which is lost: doubtless thou shalt find that they never do bring so much of commodities, but that they draw with them too too much more of incommodities and displeasures. With how painful and sore labours are they gotten, and with how great jeopardies? With how great thought and care be they kept? With how great heaviness and sorrow are they lost? which causes Christ calleth them, yea, thorns, because they rend, tear and pluck in sunder all the tranquillity and quietness of the mind, with a thousand cares, than the which tranquillity of mind, nothing is to man more sweet and pleasant, and they never quench thirst and desire of themselves, but kindleth and increaseth it more and more. They drive a man headlong into all mischief. Neither flatter thyself in vain, saying nothing forbiddeth but that a man at one time may be both rich and good. Remember what verity saith, that it is more easy for a camel to creep through the eye of a needle than a rich man to enter into the kingdom of heaven. plainly without exception true is that saying of Saint Jerome. A rich man to be either unjust himself or the heir of an unjust man: great riches can never be either gotten or else kept without sin. of how much better riches they rob thee, for he hateth the very taste and smell of virtue, he hateth all honest crafts, whosoever setteth his heart upon gold. Moreover the vice of avarice only is called idolatry of Paul. with any other vice at all Christ hath less acquaintance, neither the selfsame person can please God and mammon also.

The recapitulation of the remedies against the vice of avarice

CHAPTER XXXV

THOU shalt lightly therefore cease to wonder at money if thou wilt ponder and weigh diligently very good things with those that be false and apparent good, of painted and coloured commodities with those that be very commodities indeed. If thou wilt learn with thine inner eyes to behold and to love that noble good thing which is infinite, which only when it is present, yea though all other things should be lacking, abundantly doth satisfy the mind of man, is wider and larger of capacity than that it can be sufficed with all the good things of this world. If thou shalt oft call again before thine eyes in what condition and state thou were when the earth first received thee when thou were first born: in what state that same shall receive thee again when thou diest. If ever shall be present in thy memory that famous fool of whom is made mention in the gospel. To whom it is said: This night I will fet again thy soul from thee: and these things which thou hast gathered together, whose shall they then be? If thou shalt turn thy mind from the corrupt manners of the common sort unto the poverty of Mary, Christ's mother, unto the poverty of the apostles, of the martyrs, and most of all of Christ thy head. And set before thee that fearful word Vae, that is interpreted, woe be to you: which Christ so menaceth and threateneth unto the rich men of this world.

Against ambition or desire of honour and authority

CHAPTER XXXVI

IF at any time ambition shall cumber and vex thy mind through her enchantments, with these remedies thou shalt arm thyself beforehand without tarrying (according to the rules which I gave before), take and hold this with tooth and nail, that to be honour only which springeth of true virtue, selfsame nevertheless a man must sometime refuse, even as taught us both with doctrine and example our master Jesus Christ. this to be the chief honour and only honour which a christian man should desire and wish for, to be praised not of men, but of God, for whom he commendeth (as saith the apostle) that man is perfect and worthy of honour indeed. But if honour be given of man for an ungoodly and unhonest thing, and so of ungoodly persons: This is not honour but great dishonesty, shame and rebuke. If for any mean and indifferent thing, as for beauty, strength, riches, kin: yet verily shall it not be called truly honour, no man deserveth honour with that thing whereof he deserveth not to be praised. If for an honest thing indeed it shall be honour: yet he which deserveth it shall not desire it, but verily shall be content with the very virtue and conscience of his good deed. Behold therefore how foolish and how worthy to be laughed at these honours be, for whose desire the common people so greatly burn and rage. of all of whom are they given? Truly of them with whom is no difference between honesty and dishonesty. Wherefore are they given? Very oft for mean things, now and then for filthy things. To whom? To him which is unworthy. Whosoever therefore giveth honour, either he doth it for fear, and then is he to be feared again, or because thou wouldest do him a good turn, and then he mocketh thee: or because he is astonished at things of naught and worthy of no honour, and then he is to be pitied: or because he supposed thee to be endued with such things as honour is given of duty, wherein if he be deceived, give diligence that thou mayest be that he supposeth thee to be. But and if he hit aright, refer all the honour that is offered thee unto to whom thou art bound, yea for all those things whereunto the honour is given. As thou oughtest not ascribe to thine own self the virtue, so is it unfitting to take upon thee the honour thereof. this, what is greater madness than to esteem the value of thyself by the opinions of foolish men, in whose hands it lieth to take away again whensoever they list the very same honour which they give, and dishonest thee which was even now honested. Therefore nothing can be more foolish than either to rejoice for such honours when they happen, or to sorry or mourn when they be taken away, which not to be true honours thou shalt perceive at the least way by this probation and argument, for so much as they be common to the worst and lewdest persons of all: yea they chance almost to none more plenteously than to them which of true honours be most unworthy. how blessed is the quietness of a mean life, both private, that is to say, charged with no common business, and separate and removed out of the way from all noise, haunt, or press. On the other side consider how full of pricks, how full of cares, of perils, of sorrows, is the life of great men, and what difficulty it is not to forget thyself in prosperity, how hard it is for a man standing in a slippery place not to fall, how grievous the fall is from an high. And remember that all honour is coupled with great charge, and how strait the judgment of the high judge shall be against them which here in usurping of honours, prefer themselves afore other men. For surely whosoever shall humble and submit himself, him as an innocent or harmless person mercy shall succour: but whosoever exalteth himself as a perfect man, same person excludeth from himself the help and succour of grace. Let ever the example of Christ thy head stick fast in thy mind. What thing as touching to the world was more vile, more despised or less honoured than he? How forsook he honours when they were proffered him, which was greater than any honour? How set he no store of honours when he rode upon an ass? How condemned he them when he was clothed in pall and crowned with thorn? How unglorious or vile a death chose he? But whom the world despised him the father glorified. Let thy glory be in the cross of Christ, in whom also is thy health, wealth, saving, defence and protection. What good shall worldly honours do to thee if God cast thee away and depise thee, and the angels loathe, abhor, and defy thee?

Against elation otherwise called pride or swelling of the mind

CHAPTER XXXVII

THOU shalt not swell in thy mind if, (according to the common proverb used of every man) thou wouldest know thyself: that is whatsoever great thing, r goodly or beautiful thing, whatsoever excellent thing is in thee, thou account that to be the gift of God, and not thy good. On the other side, if whatsoever is low or vile, whatsoever is foul or filthy, whatsoever is shrewd or evil thou ascribe that altogether unto thine own self: if thou remember in how much filth thou were conceived, in how much born, how naked, how needy, how brutish, how wretched, how miserably thou creepest into this light. If thou remember into how many diseases or sickness on every side, unto how many chances, unto how many encumbrances, griefs, and troubles this wretched body is dangered. And again how little a thing were able shortly to consume and bring to naught this cruel and unruly giant, swelling with so mighty a spirit. also this, what manner thing that is whereof thou takest upon thee: if it be a mean or an indifferent thing, it is foolishness: if a filthy thing, it is madness: if an unhonest thing, it is unkindness. Remember also nothing to be a more sure document or proof of stark foolishness and lack of understanding, than if a man stand greatly in his own conceit. And again that no kind of folly is more uncurable, if thy mind begin to arise and wax great because a vile man submitteth himself to thee. Think how much greater and mightier God hangeth over thine head, which crusheth down every proud neck erect straight up, and bringeth every hill unto a plain, which spared not, no verily not so much as the angel when he was fallen into pride. And these things also shall be good though they seem somewhat as they were trifles, if thou wouldest compare thyself alway with excellent persons. Thou likest thyself because of a little beauty of thy body: compare thyself to them which in beauty be far before thee. A little cunning maketh thee to set up thy feathers, turn thine eyes unto them in comparison of whom thou mayst seem to have learned nothing at all.

Moreover if thou wilt account not how much of good things thou hast, but how much thou lackest: And with Paul, forgetful of those things which be behind thee, wouldest stretch forth thyself to those things which remain afore thee. Furthermore that also shall not be an unwise thing, if when the wind of pride doth blow, by and by we turn our very evil things into a remedy, as it were expelling one poison with another. thing shall this wise come to pass, if when any great vice or deformity of body, when any notable damage either fortune hath given, or folly hath brought to us which might gnaw us vehemently by the stomach, we set that before our eyes, and by the example of the peacock we behold ourselves chiefly in that part of us in which we be most deformed, and so shall thy feathers fall forthwith and thy pride abate. all these (besides that none other vice is more hated unto God) remember also that arrogancy, pride, and presumption is notably hated and had in derision everywhere among men: when contrariwise lowliness and meekness, both purchaseth the favour of God, and knitteth on to the benevolence of man. Therefore to speak compendiously, two things chiefly shall refrain thee from pride, if thou consider what thou art in thyself, filthy in thy birth, a bubble (such as riseth in the water) throughout all thy life, worms' meat in thy death, and what Christ was made for thee.

Against wrath and desire of vengeance

CHAPTER XXXVIII

WHEN fervent sorrow of the mind stirreth thee up unto vengeance, remember wrath to be nothing less than that which it falsely counterfeiteth, that is to wit fortitude or manfulness: for nothing is so childish, weak, nothing so feeble and of so vile a mind as to rejoice in vengeance. Thou wouldest be counted a man of great stomach, and therefore thou sufferest not injury to be unavenged: but in conclusion by this means thou utterest thy childishness, seeing thou canst not rule thine own mind, which is the very property and office of a man. How much manlier, how much excellenter it is to set another man's folly at naught than to counterfeit it? he hath hurt thee, he is proud and fierce, he scorneth thee. The filthier he is, so much the more beware lest thou be made like him. What the devil's madness is it that thou to avenge another man's lewdness wouldest be made the lewder thyself? If thou despise the rebuke, all men shall perceive that it was done to one unworthy thereof: but and if thou be moved, thou shalt make his quarrel which did the wrong much the better. Furthermore take the thing as it is, if any wrong be received, that is not eased one whit with vengeance but augmented. For in conclusion what end shall there be of injuries on both sides if every man go forth and proceed to revenge his own grief? Enemies increase on both parts, the sorrow waxeth fresh and raw again, and the longer it endureth the more uncurable it is: but with softness and with sufferance is healed now and then, yea even he which did the wrong, and after he is come to himself again, of an enemy is made a very trusty and faithful friend. But the very same hurt which by vengeance thou covetest to put from thee reboundeth back again upon thee, and not without increase of harm. And that also shall be a sovereign remedy against wrath if, according to the division of things above rehearsed, thou shouldest consider that one man cannot hurt another unless he will himself, save in those things only which be outward goods, which so greatly pertain not unto man: for the very good things of the mind God only is able to take away, which he is not wont to do but unto unkind persons, and only he can give them, which he hath not used to do unto cruel and furious persons. No christian man therefore is hurt but of himself. Injury hurteth no man but the worker thereof. These things also help (though they be not weighty) that thou shalt not follow the sorrow of thy mind: If, the circumstances of rhetoricians well gathered together, thou both make light of thine own harms, and also minish the wrong done of another man commonly after this manner: He hurt me, but it will be soon amended. Moreover he is a child, he is of things unexpert, he is a young man, it is a woman, he did it through another man's motion or counsel, he did it unaware, or when he had well drunk, it is meet that I forgive him. And on the other side he hath hurt me grievously. Certain, but he is my father, my brother, my master, my friend, my wife, it is according that this grief should be forgiven, either for the love, or else for the authority of the person. Or else thou shalt set one thing against another, and recompense the injury with other good benefits done of him unto thee. Or with thine offences done to him afore season shalt account it even, and so make quit. This man hath hurt me verily, but other times how oft hath he done me good. It cometh of an unliberal mind to forget the good benefits and only to remember a little wrong or displeasure. Now he hath offended me, but how oft offended of me. I will forgive him, that he in likewise by mine example may pardon me, if I another time trespass against him. Finally it shall be a remedy of much greater virtue and of strong operation, if in the misdoing of another man against thee thou didest think in thyself, what things, how grievous, and how oft thou hast sinned against God, how many manner of ways thou art in debt to him: as much as thou shalt remit unto thy brother which is in thy debt, much shall God forgive unto thee. This way of forgiving other men's debts hath he taught us which is himself a creditor, he will not refuse the law which he himself made. To be absolved or loosed from thy sins thou runnest to Rome, sailest to Saint James, buyest pardons most large. I dispraise not verily that thing which thou doest: but when all is done, there is no readier way, no surer means whereby (if thou have offended) thou mightest come to favour again and be reconciled to God, than if thou, when thou art offended, be reconciled again unto thy brother, forgive a little trespass unto thy neighbour (for it is but small whatsoever one man trespasseth against another) that Christ may forgive thee so many thousand offences. it is hard (thou sayest) to subdue the mind when he beginneth to wax hot. Rememberest thou not, how much harder things Christ suffered for thee? what were thou when he for thy sake bestowed his precious life? Were thou not his enemy? With what softness suffereth he the daily repeating thine old sins? Last of all how meekly suffered he the uttermost rebukes, bonds, stripes, finally death most shameful? Why? Why? Boastest thou thyself of the head, if thou care not to be in the body? Thou shalt not be a member of Christ except thou follow the steps of Christ. But he is unworthy to be forgiven. so were not thou unworthy whom God should forgive? In thine own self thou wilt have mercy exercised, and against thy brother wilt thou use extreme and cruel justice? Is it so great a thing if thou being a sinner thyself shouldest forgive a sinner, when Christ prayed his father for them which crucified him? Is it an hard thing not to strike thy brother whom thou art also commanded to love? Is it an hard thing not to pay again an evil deed, for which except thou wouldest recompense a good, thou shalt not be that toward thy fellow that Christ was toward his servant? Finally if this man be unworthy to whom for an evil turn a good should be recompensed, yet art thou worthy to do it, Christ is worthy, for whose sake it is done. But in suffering an old displeasure I call in a new, he will do injury again if he should escape unpunished for this: if without offence thou canst avoid, avoid it: if thou canst ease or remedy it, ease it: if thou canst heal a mad man, heal him, if not let him perish himself alone rather than with thee. This man which thinketh himself to have done harm, think thou worthy to be pitied, and not to be punished. Wilt thou be angry to thy commendation and laud? angry with the vice, not with the man. But the more thou art inclined by nature to this kind of vice, so much the more diligently arm thyself long beforehand, and once for altogether print sure in thy mind this decree or purpose: that thou neither say nor do anything at any time while thou art angry: believe not thyself when thou art moved: have suspected whatsoever that sudden motion or rage of the mind designeth or judgeth, yea though it be honest. none other difference to be between a frantic person and him that rageth in ire than is between a short madness that dureth but a season and a continual perseverant madness. Call to mind how many things in anger thou hast said or done worthy to be repeated, which now though in vain thou wouldest fain were changed. Therefore when that wrath waxeth hot and boileth: if thou cannot straightway save and deliver thyself altogether from anger, at the least way come thus far forth to thyself and soberness that thou remember thyself not to be well advised or in thy right mind: To remember this is a great part of health. On this wise reason with thyself, now verily so am I minded, but anon hereafter I shall be of another mind much contrary, why should I in the mean season say against my friend (while I am moved) that thing which hereafter when I am appeased and my malice ceased I could not change: why should I now do in my malice or anger that thing which when I am sobered and come to myself again I should greatly sorrow and repent. Why rather should not reason, why should not pity, at the last why should not Christ obtain that of me now, which a little pause of time shall shortly hereafter obtain. To no man (I suppose) hath nature given so much of black colour but at the least way he might so far forth rule himself. it shall be a very good thing for thee thus instructed to harden thy mind with reason, with continuance and custom that thou couldest not be moved at all: it shall be a perfect thing, if thou, having indignation only at the vice, for a displeasure or rebuke done to thee, shalt render again a deed of charity. To conclude, even natural temperance, which ought to be in every man, requireth that thou shouldst not suffer affections to rule thee utterly. Not to be wroth at all is a thing most like unto God, and therefore most comely and beautiful. To overcome evil with goodness, malice with kindness, is to counterfeit the perfect charity of Christ Jesu. To hold wrath under and keep him back with a bridle is the property of a wise man. To follow the appetite of wrath is not a point of a man verily, but plainly of beasts, and that of wild beasts. But if thou wouldest know how much uncomely it were to a man to be overcome with wrath, look when thou art sober that thou mark the countenance of an angry person, or else when thou thyself art angry, go unto a glass. thine eyes so burn flaming in fire, when thy cheeks be pale, when thy mouth is drawn awry, thy lips foam, all thy members quake, when thy voice soundeth so maliciously, neither thy gestures be of one fashion, who would judge thee to be a man?

Thou perceivest now my most sweetest friend how large a sea is open all abroad to dispute of other vices after this same manner. But we in the midst of our course will strike sail leaving the rest to thy discretion. Neither certain was it my mind, purpose, or intention (for that should be an infinite work) as I began, even so to dissuade thee from every vice, vice by vice, as it were with sundry declamations, to bold and courage thee to the contrary virtues. This only was my desire (which I thought sufficient for thee) to shew a certain manner and craft of a new kind of war, how thou mightest arm thyself against the evils of the old life burgeoning forth again and springing afresh. Therefore as we have done in one or two things (because of example) so must thou thyself do partly in everything, one by one: but most of all in the things whereunto thou shalt perceive thyself to be stirred or instigate peculiarly, whether it be through vice of nature, custom, or evil bringing up, against these things some certain decrees must be written in the table of thy mind, they must be renewed now and then, lest they should fail or be forgotten through disuse, as against the vices of backbiting, filthy speaking, envy, guile, and other like: these be the only enemies of Christ's soldiers, against whose assault the mind must be armed long aforehand with prayer, with noble sayings of wise men, with the doctrine of holy scripture, with example of devout and holy men, and specially of Christ. Though I doubt not but that the reading of holy scripture shall minister all these things to thee abundantly, nevertheless charity which one brother oweth to another hath moved and exhorted me that at the least way with this sudden and hasty writings, I should further and help thy holy purpose as much as lieth in me: a thing which I have done somewhat the rather because I somewhat feared lest thou shouldest fall into that superstitious kind of religious men, partly awaiting on their own advantage, partly with great zeal, but not according to knowledge, walk round about both by sea and land, and if anywhere they get a man recovering from vices unto virtue, him straightway with most importune and lewd exhortations, threatenings, and flatterings they enforce to thrust into the order of monks, even as though without a cowl there were no christendom. re when they have filled his breast with pure scrupulosity and doubts insoluble, then they bind him to certain traditions found by man, and plainly thrust the wretched person headlong into a certain bondage of ceremonies like unto the manner of the Jews, and teach him to tremble and fear, but not to love. order of monkship is not piety, but a kind of living to every man after the disposition of his body and his mind, also either profitable or unprofitable, whereunto verily as I do not courage thee, so likewise I counsel not from it. This thing only I warn thee of, that thou put piety neither in meat nor in raiment or habit, nor in any visible thing, but in those things which have been declared and shewed thee afore: and in whatsoever persons thou shalt find or perceive the true image of Christ, with them couple thyself. Moreover when such men be lacking whose conversation should make thee better, withdraw thyself as much as thou mayst from the company of man, call the holy prophet, Christ and the apostles unto communication, but specially make Paul of familiar acquaintance with thee. This fellow must be had ever in thy bosom to be read and studied both night and day: finally and to be learned without the book word by word, upon whom we have now a good while enforced with great diligence to make a comment or a narration, a bold deed truly. But notwithstanding we, trusting in the help of God, will endeavour ourself busily, lest after Origene, Ambrose, and Augustyne, lest after so many new interpreters we should seem to have taken this labour upon us utterly either without a cause or without fruit: and also that certain busy and unquiet pick-quarrels, which think it perfect religion to know nothing at all of good learning, may understand and well perceive that whereas we in youth have embraced and made much of the pure learning of old authors, and also have gotten, and that not without great sweat and watch, a mean understanding of both the tongues Greke and Latyn. have not in so doing looked unto a vain and foolish fame, or unto the childish pastime and pleasure of our mind, but that we were minded long before to adorn and garnish the Lord's temple with the riches of other strange nations and countries to the uttermost of our power. Which temple some men with their ignorance and barbarousness hath overmuch dishonested, that by the reason of such riches excellent wits might also be inflamed unto the love of holy scripture. But this so great a thing a few days laid apart, we have taken upon us this labour for thy sake, that unto thee (as it were with a finger) we might shew the way which leadeth straight unto Christ. And I beseech Jesu the father of this holy purpose (as I hope) that he would vouchsafe benignly to favour thy wholesome enforcements, yea that he would in changing of thee increase his grace, and make thee perfect, that thou mightest quickly wax big and strong in him, and spring up unto a perfect man. In whom also fare thou well, brother and friend, always verily beloved in my heart, but now much more than before both dear and plesant. At the town of Saint Andomers, the year of Christ's birth 1501.

Here endeth this book called Enchiridion or the manual of the Christian knight, made by Erasmus of Roterdame, in the which book is contained many goodly lessons very necessary and profitable for the soul's health of all true Christian people: Imprinted at London by Wynkyn de Worde, for Johan Byddell, otherwise Salisbury, the xv. day of Novembre. And be for to sell at the sign of our Lady of pytie next to Flete Bridge.

1533.

Cum privilegio regali.

25370546R00097

Made in the USA
Middletown, DE
28 October 2015